To M⟨...⟩

Best Wishes,
John Savage, CM

"Before one speaks, he
should be sure that it is going
to improve upon the silence."

It's Getting Easier

JOHN SAVAGE, CLU

THE NATIONAL UNDERWRITER COMPANY
CINCINNATI, OHIO

First Edition
Fourth Printing
1986

Printed in the United States of America

Library of Congress Catalogue Card Number: 80-81887

International Standard Book Number: 0-87218-010-7

DEDICATION

I would like to dedicate this book to my family. My wife, Kate—wonder woman. She accomplishes more in one week than most people do in one month. After observing her for 21 years, I still am awed by her accomplishments. She is truly my backbone.

To son John: It is a real blessing from Almighty God to have your Number One son turn out with his head on straight after 20 years; for that, I say "thanks."

To Kevin: Blessed with intelligence and personality, his future is whatever he wants it to be.

To Jeff: The all-around athlete who has participated in four sports in high school. He's a true joy to all who know him well.

To Scott: Although John, Jeff, and Kevin all played varsity basketball, this young man entered high school this year with the most God-given talent and should really provide his parents with exciting days ahead on the baseball diamond, the basketball floor, at piano recitals, and hopefully, with high academic marks as well.

To Brian: Mr. Excitement and Attitude. It's a shame that Brian has to sleep because he is worth watching 24 hours a day. Loaded with enthusiasm and maybe the Number One achiever, he also is helped with many God-given intellectual endowments.

To Patti: Finally, we get to the girls! She's the reader of the family. I sincerely believe that Patti would be happy if she read all day long. But she also packs an enthusiastic personality into an intelligently designed life pattern. She loves sports, piano, but more . . . she loves life.

v

To Kelly: Maybe the best athlete in the family, only time will tell. "Miss Empathy" would be the name to best tell the story of Kelly. She truly cares for other people, deeply. She likes to play the guitar, but doesn't like to practice.

To Sean: His goal is to be the best basketball player in the family and I tell him it's a nice goal. But both Kate and I would like to see him have the same goals in the classroom because at this moment, we feel that God has given him much, and educationally, not all the debts are being paid.

To Aaron: Keeps us all busy as most five-year-olds do. He is a real companion for brother Sean, and promises he will be a good boy.

ABOUT THE AUTHOR

John Savage comes from Toledo, Ohio, where until 1976, he was head of the leading agency for Columbus Mutual Life. He is a Life and Qualifying member of the Million Dollar Round Table, and last year he produced in excess of $14 million of personal business.

While his business is selling life insurance, his avocation for the last several years has been speaking—an activity which he enjoys immensely, particularly when he is helping young people in life insurance sales. He has been a featured speaker at the annual meetings of both the Million Dollar Round Table and the National Association of Life Underwriters, and has addressed more than 200 sales congresses and meetings in the United States, Great Britain, Canada, Australia, and the Dominican Republic. John has also authored, *The Easy Sale*, which is available from The National Underwriter Company.

John graduated from the University of Toledo in 1952 and has been chairman of the university board of trustees. He is active in the business community of Toledo and serves on numerous boards of directors.

John is age 50 and he and his wife, Kate, have seven sons and two daughters.

Cincinnati, Ohio
June, 1980

AUTHOR'S PREFACE

Why a second book? There are probably four reasons. First, the many letters and phone calls I received after *The Easy Sale* was published. It was very gratifying that so many people seemed to have enjoyed the first book and improved their sales with the application of its ideas.

More than that, however, there were the many people who said they found a degree of tranquility offered by some of the simple examples and philosophy on life itself, *for example,* attitude.

Second, I became painfully aware, after talking to many frustrated agents who have been doing what has been taught for years, that new and creative ideas are needed, ones that can excite the salesman's mind, and generate enthusiasm that will bring about a higher rate of productivity.

Thirdly, there is a fair amount of enjoyment that comes with the knowledge that people are reading and applying your ideas.

Lastly, I am not a good writer. However, while I have spoken to many groups, I find a book is the only way to leave material that will last.

An additional consideration, too, since I'm reducing the number of my industry speaking engagements, is that this book, and *The Easy Sale* will be my communication to those people I will never have the opportunity to meet in person.

John Savage, CLU

Toledo, Ohio
June, 1980

TABLE OF CONTENTS

Chapter 1
IT'S GETTING EASIER

It's Getting Easier may seem to be an over-simplification for a title, but believe me, it simply will happen. Many young people in this business have heard me say that all you have to do to make it is last. There's a little more to it, but consider these facts:

—Most experienced agents make fewer calls than the younger agents.

—Most experienced agents sell most of their business to old policyholders, or to referrals from their old policyholders.

—Almost all men and women agree *that the business gets easier* for those two reasons.

There's no possible way that I can *instantly* advance a young agent to this stage, but I can tell that person there is something to look forward to down the road.

It is easier for a shortstop to go after a ground ball after eight years in the majors than it was in his rookie year.

A majorette will tell you that it isn't nearly as tough in her senior year to perform before a packed stadium as it was on that first sunny day in fall when she was a freshman.

You will say that's all about building dexterity, and you're right. But I believe it's also about building confidence.

There could be exceptions. Perhaps the President of the United States finds each year more difficult than the last because of the accumulation of new problems and the tremendous pressures of the office. However, he might tell you too, that experience has in many instances made matters easier to decide.

1

I selected "It's Getting Easier" to give new agents some reason to look ahead. They are confronted by so many prophets of doom and gloom and so many promises, that never are kept by supervisors, it is no wonder they have difficulty in keeping a positive attitude.

In 1951, when I began this business, it did not have the best reputation. Sure, we were a notch or two above a snake oil salesman, but several degrees below the public image of a lawyer or physician.

Woody Allen, in one of his movies a few years ago, got a huge laugh during one scene where he was working on a chain gang. He was sentenced to three weeks in prison for bad behavior with a life insurance salesman.

In the last several years the life insurance agent has made monumental progress. I think, by comparison, we now have a better public reputation then either a doctor or a lawyer. Twenty-five years ago, both professions were revered. Today, the thinking public is questioning and evaluating them with the same diligence it applies to individuals in other professions. Within the next 25 years, I believe we will be considered true professionals.

During the '60's we had to live with the mutual fund expert who told the buyer to buy term insurance and invest the difference for mutual funds *almost* guaranteed a 10 to 15 per cent return. Unfortunately, many people were left holding the bag with their investments and the representative who sold the funds did not survive in the business of selling them. In other words, when purchasing life insurance, there is more to consider than dollars and cents. A little later I'll elaborate on this point.

I am persuaded that most people are far better off with the selection of a solid agent who is going to grow and progress and who has the client's interest at heart than they are with the

2

Number Three company from a net cost standpoint. I've often said that you are are better off with the Number One agent from the worst company than you are with the worst agent from the Number One net cost company.

Selling will be easier as the practitioner, as with the shortstop in baseball, developes selling skills. Encompassed in this is a philosophy and psychology that I try to give to the buyer.

In my earlier selling years I was trying to develop a clientele while also trying to develop as a human being—and this is a much harder and unending job, I believe. I have found, too, that most of my clients want to become better persons and, in many instances, are looking for psychological balance.

No reader, I believe, will disagree that attaining this is the ultimate in happiness. That's why most people are searching for psychological balance.

Truly there is a need in this area. We help meet the need when, as human beings, we help other persons who are confronted with the troubles that grow out of imbalance.

If it is true that people seek psychological equilibrium, and I'm sure it is, it follows as well that most people would be happier with financial balance.

An agent in our business must acknowledge that. He must consider the buyer's whole financial situation rather than seeking him out when the company has a sales contest to sell life insurance policies.

Today's buyer wants trust, and building a trust is probably the most important ability you can develop and cultivate for successful selling.

3

Trust is all we have in dealing with one another. Once we violate that trust we have nothing. Each individual who is being sold looks for someone to believe in 100 per cent.

Often, I have stated that people don't buy insurance. People buy people! Let's talk about this.

All of us are looking for people with whom we can trust in both business as well as in personal friendships. We seek this whether we are looking for a builder for our new home, or for a dentist who is going to take care of our family. If we must have a major operation, we want a top physician who can perform to our satisfaction. Seldom is cost taken into consideration when making these decisions.

Integrity is what we want when searching out the dentist, the doctor or the homebuilder. So when you, the insurance agent, go out each day to sell, please understand that the buyer is looking for a quality individual and not for someone offering a product with the lowest price.

The buyer of our services doesn't have cost as the top priority. He's looking for someone who will provide service to meet certain needs, who has understanding, and who is an able person whose first concern is the buyer. All of us make promises. Are we giving what we have promised?

Years ago, when we were younger, Hopalong Cassidy was a television show sponsored by a popular breakfast cereal. One of the promises held out in the commerical was, "If you want to be like Hoppy, then you gotta eat like Hoppy."

Well, all of you who are trying to become professionals in this business—start acting like a professional and perform to the satisfaction of your clients. No one will be satisfied with a poor performance. When you examine agents who continue to make gains in productivity, you will find their biggest gains,

4

in their relationships with clients, have been made behind the scenes.

Yes, *it's getting easier,* but it will not and never will be easier for the person who hasn't paid his dues with intellectual honesty, and who hasn't tried to learn all that is possible about our business.

Chapter 2
WHY IT'S EASIER

The spotlight focuses on center stage. The singer starts. Halfway through the performance the microphone goes dead! He laughs, but keeps on singing. All of a sudden, everyone is cheering for the entertainer!

If you are a younger person calling on an older prospect most people are pulling for you. The veteran often gets a kick when you have the guts to tackle the subject matter with the prospect. If everyone understood this then law, teaching and most work, including selling of life insurance, would be getting easier.

There are some conditions now, too, that are working in your favor, like:

—Buyer awareness

—Inflation (really!)

—Institutionalizing of fringe benefits

—Women in business

Consider yourself for a minute. You probably know more today than you did a few years ago. You're better educated in the field, and if you're working and reading, meeting people, and attending the Million Dollar Round Table every year, if you're rubbing shoulders with the best performers, you're going to gain more knowledge.

I've often said that in selling knowledge of the product is 5 per cent, knowledge of people is 95 per cent. But naturally, you have to know as much as possible about that 5 per cent.

The longer you are in the business, the better equipped you'll be in your daily sales endeavors.

And when you know, other people know that you know!

You're wired together and the voltage is 220. Don't short-change the buyer! I have the feeling that the buyer has been underestimated for centuries.

People have keen insights into another's knowledge. Yes, there are people fooled every day, but across the board, I'll bet it won't be for any great length of time.

Communicate! I tell my children the best education they could have would be a course on mastering two books, the Bible and the dictionary. If you could do that, your sales potential certainly would be enhanced.

The ability to communicate and to have a good vocabulary at your fingertips is crucial. An English background is very important. It can help you learn how to speak with language that is easy on the ear.

Most schools, both public and private, do a very poor job preparing people in communications skills. They under-emphasize it. In high school I had one semester of public speaking and six of math. Don't you believe it should have been the other way around?

People who excel in the communicating arts seem to do well in any field. In contrast, if you are a general contractor and you can't communicate, you probably aren't going to be very successful.

You must build trust. Once you have built trust with your client, man or woman, you will find that client coming to you for any additional needs and problems that need solutions.

Building your clientele makes it easier. This year I'm planning to sell $15 million. I can't imagine that someone starting out in this business could look at such a goal. It would be too mind-boggling.

Yet, I can see $20 million as a personal reality. And I think that personal reality is shared by a number of people who are today selling in the neighborhood of $10 million because they know the phenomenon of gradual growth.

To some of the specifics.

The buyer is more aware—far more aware—of the importance of having life insurance than he was 25 years ago.

At one time many people considered group insurance to be total coverage. They never bought any personal life insurance, didn't have a lot of dollars, and the limit on their pocketbook was the limit on their ability to buy.

As incomes began to grow, social demands on the pocketbook became a reality, and so has a greater opportunity to set priorities on your expenses.

You know this is so because you're really considering whether to buy a third or fourth television set or a third car, instead of being limited to one car and a single television after you buy food and clothing.

It's far easier to argue that it is more important to give protection to your family, whether both parents are working or not, than it is to consider buying a third car.

This is the kind of logic I'm talking about.

If you are talking to a father with children it's pretty logical to talk to him about protecting them.

Inflation has become, in the broad sense, a major plus for the sale of life insurance. When you are talking to people whose incomes now are not uncommonly $20,000, $30,000, $40,000 and upwards to $100,000, there's more need to increase coverage to protect that income and for a greater number of years.

It is easier now, in a sales presentation, to introduce the idea of greater amounts of coverage. Twenty years ago, you sold a policy on the life of a wife to bury her. Grim thought, but correct. Not that it was the design of the marriage, since she wasn't a working person, but the couple didn't figure her human life value to be high.

We all know that's not the case today. Even with women who do not work, but who take care of four or five children, there is a greater realization of the great economic loss that would result if they died. Consider the costs of day care alone! The need for wife insurance and mother insurance really has come into being.

Many new businesses are started and require great capital investment and produce huge debt—certainly more now than in previous years. The individual who starts a business requires more coverage on his life in case he does not live long enough to liquidate the debt requirement. Lending institutions have been insisting on this coverage and that's helped our business, too. All these factors are catalysts which makes our business easier.

Fringe benefits, group insurance, and all the extras that really are no longer "extras" in a so-called employee wage package have made more people more cognizant of the need for insurance.

That awareness alone makes the selling of life insurance today a better career than it was. Those who have fringe benefits certainly aren't going to tell you they don't believe in them.

10

Rather, they'll tell you most fringe benefit packages lag behind the need. People who rely strictly on fringe benefits and social security do not leave their family well cared for when they die.

Better competition in the field is making the business easier, too. Why is that? Consider this.

A new Burger King restaurant builds right next to a McDonald's rather than 17 blocks away. Then along comes a Kentucky Fried Chicken, then a Wendy's and a Pizza Hut, and pretty soon there are 13 fast food restaurants in two blocks. It's exemplified in Toledo, in nearby Maumee, and all over. It happens because business begets business.

The higher caliber individual being attracted to our field today is making competition keener, and I'll bet making business better because the reputation of the business will be enhanced. Clients will know their agent is a qualified individual, and someone they can do business with.

Years ago, barbers sold insurance as a part-time job, so did milkmen and school teachers. Selling life insurance today is a great career, and the acceptance by the public should make a person proud to be in the business.

So, *it's getting easier* for John Savage, but is it easier for the new person in the business? Yes and no!

Yes, for the reasons I've just given, and no, if some of the pitfalls which I discussed in *The Easy Sale* are not overcome.*
I talked about trying to learn more about yourself, liking what you are, the importance of industry, of self-discipline, of love and integrity.

Attitude is a tool of the successful salesman, one that will help minimize fears, dispel some myths, and push numerous

*Chapter One: The Man In Every Salesman

barriers out of the way. Someone once said, "It's not your aptitude, but your attitude that determines your altitude."

I believe you have to be bright, industrious, and have guts. If you have two out of three, you'll fail. If you're bright, and a gutty person, but you don't work, you'll go belly up. If you're a bright person who works hard, but you lack the courage to face people and involve yourself in selling, you won't make it either.

Move it around any way you wish.

I think the missing characteristic in most sales failures is the lack of guts. If you still have a major stumbling block to making sales easier, you might take a hard look and see if this is the problem.

Don't think for a minute that you don't have to work, and don't have to have guts and brains, because there are more areas to work in now and more people working.

Here's something that concerns me. I believe that once an individual has learned and honed his skills, he has an obligation to society, and it's *not* to retire. Yet, this is what's happening!

A lot of people who have been in the business as long as I have are working only two or three hours a day because they feel their incomes are high enough. I wonder if they understand their physchological makeup?

All of us need work to maintain a balance. We should enjoy whatever we decide to do, and if we enjoy something, we should want to do more of it.

If someone has the ability to serve, and because of experience is better equipped to provide service, that person has an obligation to serve more people.

Serving the classes is lucrative, and perhaps less time-consuming than serving the masses. Some agents say they will only spend time with clients who earn $50,000 a year or more. This bothers me. The masses of our society should have the same advantage of having a skilled producer sit down and talk to them about financial planning as the classes.

Continual work is continual growth. Anyone who thinks the same today as he or she did a year ago is not growing. And if we cannot grow and share that growth with other people, we cannot hope to assume a leadership role.

I think that's my charge: to take you from the starting blocks of business to the point where you can be a successful salesperson. And I do mean *salesperson*.

Our business is changing. Women have been in the real estate business for years where I'll bet they outsell men. Why shouldn't they do well in the insurance business? I honestly believe that a woman at a younger age is better disciplined than a man, and has a superior sensitivity level.

In the following chapters we are going to give you a lot of sales ideas but don't stop what you're doing. Don't stop what your home office believes to be important in your training. Add to it.

Too many people doing a pretty good job using *Idea A* come across *Idea B*, think it's the greatest thing invented since sliced bread, and quit doing *A*. Pretty soon, what they were doing that had been feeding them and giving them a good living is gone. With that base gone, they get discouraged.

A person earning $30,000 a year wants to make $100,000. He says, "Boy, I want to be like Ron Barbaro or Lyle Blessman," but he isn't comfortable that way. However, if you don't believe in yourself, probably it will be unanimous.

But, we're talking about reputation and character, too. Reputation is what other people think of you, and character is what you are. If you try to build your integrity and character, the reputation—and the business—will come.

Please, never sacrifice character and integrity for a big reputation.

Richard Cory

WHENEVER Richard Cory went down town,
We people on the pavement looked at him:
He was a gentleman from sole to crown,
Clean favored, and imperially slim.

And he was always quietly arrayed,
And he was always human when he talked;
But still he fluttered pulses when he said,
"Good-morning," and he glittered when he walked.

And he was rich—yes, richer than a king—
And admirably schooled in every grace:
In fine, we thought that he was everything
To make us wish that we were in his place.

So on we worked, and waited for the light,
And went without the meat, and cursed the bread;
And Richard Cory, one calm summer night,
Went home and put a bullet through his head.

Edwin Arlington Robinson

Chapter 3
SELLING IN THE 1980's

The setting for the interview is my office. A doctor, with whom I have had a breakfast or luncheon appointment, is comfortably seated with his wife in front of a large chalkboard. I start as follows:

"Doctor, you don't know me from a bottle of Vicks, but we have met. I want to go over some basic ideas and I think you are going to find this interview extremely interesting and very valuable and different than any you have had until now. You are a practicing physician. I'm a financial doctor ... no one likes the procedure but everyone likes the end results.

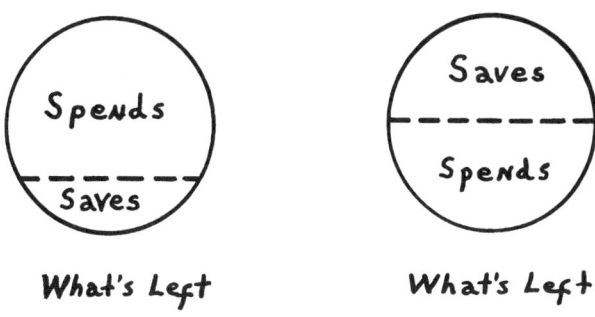

What's Left   What's Left

"There are four kinds of people: the uninformed incompetent, the uninformed competent, the informed incompetent, and the informed competent. Now, you understand that everyone falls into one of those four groups. Among those four types are two economic groups. In all of society everyone falls into one of these two circles. There are people that spend and save what is left and a very few people who save and spend what is left. Please! Listen, very carefully because I am about to give you the most powerful phrase that I have ever uttered in my entire life and maybe the most powerful phrase you have ever heard. (Pointing to the circle on the left) These people, those who spend and then save what is left always work for these people (pointing to circle on the right). Now, which group would you like to be in?"

"On the right."

"Of course. There are a whole lot of people that want to be in this group of savers but they don't know how to get there."

"I'm going to give you a seven circle presentation that is going to bring all of this out and it will show you why people don't end up in that circle."

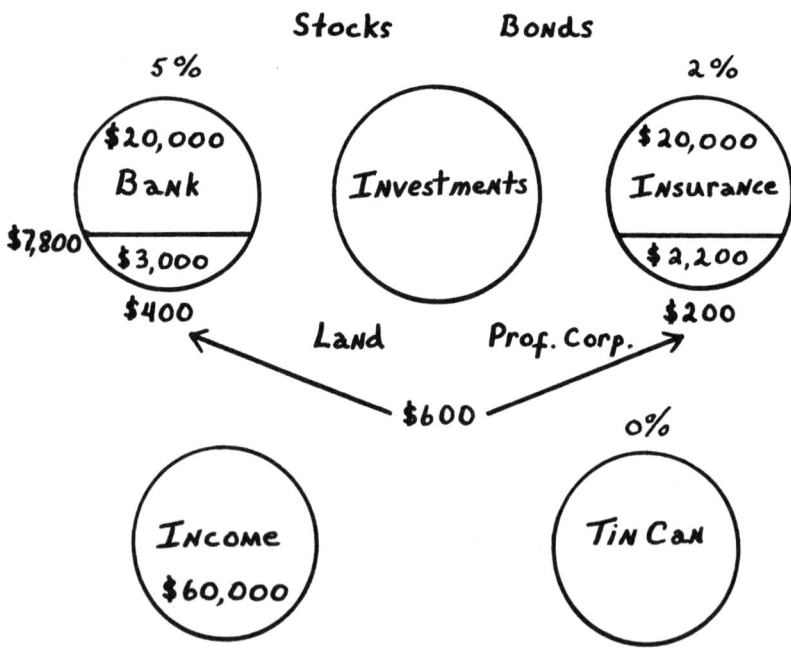

(When I first prepared this presentation I drew the circles as I proceeded. Today I prepare all seven whose titles are readily understood by the prospect with the exception of human life value. It saves time.)

"Let me explain, nothing happens until you have income. You are a pediatrician. What's your adjusted gross income after expenses?"

"$60,000." (Enter amount inside of Income circle.)

"Few people talk about this but the most important facet in financial planning is a bank account. Now, I don't work for a bank . . . I'm not a teller, but I believe we must go directly from income to the bank. The bank is a savings vehicle. Insurance is a savings vehicle. Investments are as noted, investment. Stocks (write in, etc.), bonds, land and buildings, and in your case, your pension plan and profit sharing plan with your professional corporation. There isn't anything else to talk about in financial planning. Everything will be related to one of those four things in investment and there are only a couple of saving vehicles that you should bother with, at least there are only a couple with which I bother.

"Let's talk about these vehicles. A bank account pays 5% to 6% (sometimes more), insurance pays 2%, this is what I have found as my average. If you are going to be a client of mine, I want you to get $20,000 in the bank (write this sum in Bank circle). Eventually, I want $20,000 to be in insurance cash values (write this sum in Insurance circle) but in this, the insurance, I am not in a hurry, but this (point to the Bank circle) is one of immediacy. Let me explain the difference between these two saving vehicles.

"What's the difference between 5% and 2%?"

"3%."

"Arithmetically correct but in savings the difference between 5% and 2% is zero. Now, you are going to say, I don't understand that and you are the first person to ever tell me that. But I told you that I studied this for seven years. Let me explain and we will now use the tin can. That's why it's here. Would you agree the tin can pays zero?"

"Yes."

"You can put your money there, correct?"

"Right."

"It is a savings vehicle. You can pump all kinds of money in there and people do. The tin can pays zero. The difference between 5% and 2% is zero. Now why?

"Doc, let me ask you. If you put a thousand dollars a month in the bank and a thousand dollars a month in insurance and a thousand dollars a month in a tin can, at the end of five years, where would you have the most money, if in fact, listen closely now, when the money went into the tin can it went into a vice. Every time you put the thousand in, WOMP, you couldn't get at it; next month, a thousand, WOMP, you couldn't get it. Since you have open accessibility to these two other accounts, at the end of five years, where would you have the most money?"

"In the tin can."

"In the tin can. So, the success or failure of a savings account is not predicated on the rate of return but rather on the systematic methodology of putting money into the account.

"My savings account goes like this (draw a jagged line to the left of the Bank circle), your's goes like this too, everybody's goes like this. Sure, there's the one per cent whose account doesn't . . . but we ain't talking to those people. Doc, you at thirty-five years of age—how much money do you have in the bank?"

"$3,000." (Write $3,000 in bottom of Bank circle.)

"You know all the economists, those super economists and financial wizards, as I call them, are telling people that you don't get a good return (point to Bank circle) and they are talking about the 5% of your money. Nobody talks about the 95% that you are spending. The greatest time to save money is during inflationary times, if you don't want to live like everybody else is living. If you want to eat out four days a week and you want to buy a big car and you want a new house and you want a cottage, and you want a boat; nobody talks about that. Everybody talks about where the five per cents are going. I talk about the discipline required to move some of that 95% into the bank. Obviously, up to now, you had the same problem that I had. (I tell everyone this story.) Three years ago, my wife's credit card was stolen, a month later I caught the guy but I didn't turn him in; he was spending less than she did. We all get the same social demands on our pocketbook but I am a guy that is addressing myself and you to understand the problem, that's the psychology of finance that nobody talks about. Now, I told you that this (point to Bank circle) is one of immediacy.

"How much cash value do you have in life insurance (now we look over the policies; it doesn't take three days, it takes three minutes) . . . I find that you have $2,200. (Write $2,200 in bottom of Insurance circle.) Yes, Doctor, and Mrs. Doctor, if you wanted $2,200, we could write you a check for $2,200. That is a savings but don't think of it as an expense. But answer me, honestly, what do you think about when an insurance bill comes?"

"It's an expense, it's a bill."

"It's a bill, not savings, but maybe it's the best one that you have because it is going to increase and go up every year. But, let's forget about this, let's concentrate on this (point to Bank circle) because we have to get to $20,000.

"Now, Doc, can you save $1,000 a month at the bank?"

"Hell no! I can't save that."

(How do I know he can't save a $1,000 a month at the bank? Just by the way he said "no!" I don't need a book on how to overcome objections. I want him as a client and I want him to be comfortable.)

"Can you save $800?"

"No, John, I can't."

"Can you save $600?"

"$600 a month, I think we could do that if we put discipline in our system." (Write $600 under the Investment circle.)

"See Doctor, Mrs. Doctor, the beautiful thing about the way I operate is that you are going to be back here next year. Remember, these are goals. If you don't make them, you are not going to be thrashed. I'm going to act as a catalytic agent to help you understand that you cannot go on after many years of practice with $3,000 in the bank, not when you're make $60,000. I'm only going to be around to help you. I can't dictate that you get that done but I know that if we meet every year and when your total financial picture is put up here (point to diagram), you're going to get excited about where you are going and I am going to be that catalyst.

"What I would like for you to do the first year is take $400 of this money and move it over here (draw a line from under the $600 to the Bank circle, put an arrowhead on line just below Bank circle, write $400 at low point of line) so that next year when we get together there is going to be $7,800 there ($3,000 + 12 x $400) (write $7,800 to left of circle), and we will be well along our way to your goal. Keep in mind, I look at this as a three-year goal.

"Once we get $20,000 in there, we are going to move $10,000 of it over to investments. If you are going to make strides in our capitalistic system you ultimately must get into this circle (point to Investment circle). This part is already blown-up by you breathing and going to work . . . your pension and profit sharing plans. While this circle is the last one that you should consider, we must get in there because this is where percentages and returns mean something. We're building the foundation for what, the investment. This isn't the house (point to Bank circle), this is the foundation. Here is the house, the financial planning house is investment. Ultimately, this is where we have to direct all our attention.

"If we put $400 over here, I want to put $200 over here (draw a line from under the $600 to the Insurance circle, put an arrowhead on line just below Insurance circle) so that next year when you come here there will be $5,000 sitting in there."

(How do I know there is going to be $5,000? The cash values in the old policies are going to increase which has nothing to do with the new premium money. I'm going to do a financial planning job for them and at this point I don't know how much of the $200 is going to go for protection, term insurance, or for permanment.)

(This is powerful! I always say this.)

"Does any of this make sense?"

"Yes!"

(They always say "yes." I would like to say they don't. "John, I'm asked, what do you say if they say 'no'?" They never do. I think you sell yourself in the first interview so the prospect is comfortable when he or she comes to your office.)

21

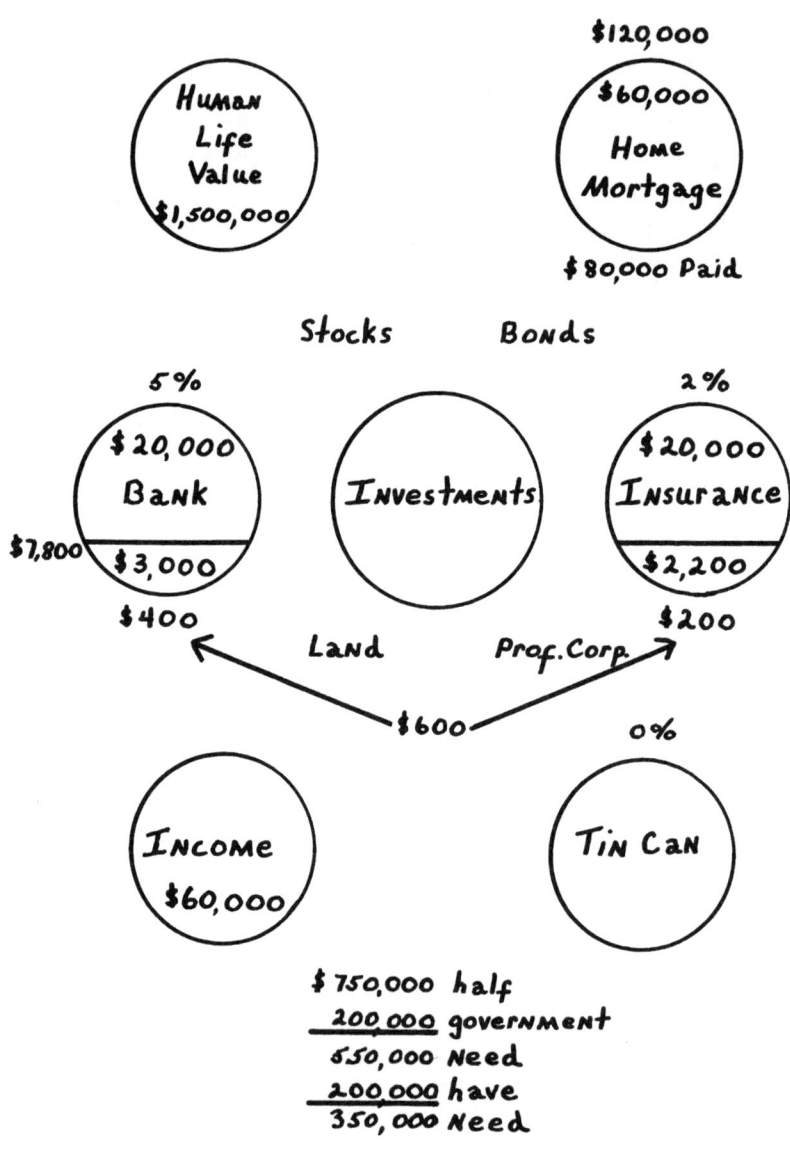

Human Life Value $1,500,000

$120,000
$60,000
Home Mortgage
$80,000 Paid

Stocks   Bonds

5%   2%
$20,000   Investments $20,000
Bank   Insurance
$7,800 | $3,000 $2,200
$400 $200

Land   Prof. Corp.
$600   0%

Income $60,000   Tin Can

$750,000 half
 200,000 government
 550,000 Need
 200,000 have
 350,000 Need

"Now, I really want to open your eyes (we call this advanced underwriting) because we're going to have fun over the next five or ten years. After five years you probably won't need me because the job will be done. Since we're creatures of habit once we start formulating something it will become part of us. I don't want a disciple, I don't want you doing what I do, but I want to show you what I am doing because I'm having fun. Then you can take what you like and discard what you don't like ... the basic thing is for you to be comfortable.

"Now, do you have a home?"

"Yes."

"What's your home worth?"

"$120,000." (Write $120,000 above Home circle.)

"What did you pay for it?"

"$80,000." (Write $80,000 Paid below Home circle.)

"What's the mortgage?"

"$60,000." (Write $60,000 Mortgage inside Home circle.)

"How much fire insurance do you have on the home?"

"$120,000."

"You've got to be kidding?" (I always say that.)

"Yes, I have that much. What do you mean?"

"I'll come to that in a minute ... you're 35 years of age, your income is $60,000 a year; if you never get a raise and if you work until age 60, your human life value is $1,500,000 (write $1,500,000 inside Human Life Value circle). If I told you that you should buy $1,500,000 worth of life insurance you would say, 'John, you need a treatment. We're going to take you to the local hospital and we'll get a top psychologist. Since I'm a doctor I know lots of them . . . you're in deep trouble.' But the casualty agent over here (point to the House circle) called on the telephone and said, 'Doc, do you realize, because of inflation, the value of your house has gone from $80,000 to $120,000 and for $40 a month you can increase your coverage,' and you said, 'Put it on!' You don't need $1,500,000 of life insurance, but is it asking too much for you to consider one-half?'' (Write $750,000 Half, at bottom of chart between the Income and Tin Can circles.)

"You mean, buy $750,000?"

"Heck, no." (How do I know this? Just the way he said 'buy' and I don't want my clients to be uncomfortable.)

The government thinks enough of you that they have $200,000 of decreasing term on you and they call it Social Security (write $200,000 Government, below $750,000 Half. It doesn't make any difference if it is $200,000, $220,000 or $230,000. You can work all those things out. I'm not talking about exactness, I'm talking about a philosophy.)

"You only need $550,000 (write $550,000 Need, below $200,000 Government) and you already own $200,000 (write $200,000 Have, below $550,000 Need), so that means you need $350,000 (complete the mathematics) and you can get it for $200 a month.

Once you follow the formula and if you die tomorrow, your wife gets $60,000 a year for the rest of her life. In programming, getting up-to-date in the eighties, if you die making $60,000, you should leave $60,000, otherwise you have absconded. These income formulas used by many people escape me.

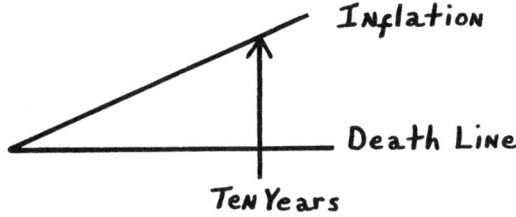

Inflation

Death Line

Ten Years

"Why should you leave $60,000? That's the death line (write Death Line to right of bottom side of angle). If you're dead, you're dead a long time, right?"

"Right."

"Here is inflation (write Inflation to right of top side of angle). Ten years after you are dead (write Ten Years below angle and draw a line between the sides of the angle with an arrowhead touching the top side of the angle) your wife and family may need $60,000 just to eat. So, we never, ever can settle for less than insuring the living benefit. Sure, Social Security is going to increase but it's always behind and it's not overly funded. If you die with $550,000 of life insurance, coupled with Social Security and your other values that you have here (point to Investments), your wife is going to have that income and she is never going to deplete the principal.

(We can get 9%, we can get 10% . . . we can do a lot of things. At this point we get conservative and we help him; we can move to a trust if he doesn't have a trust. We may do a lot of things but the big thing is that I have his commitment that he has gone along for $200 a month. The $200 will buy some ordinary life and some term.)

"Next year, when you come back, we are going to evaluate where you are going. I'm going to tell you something now. In my opinion, Doc, you have all the life insurance that you will ever need. If anyone calls you up and tells you that you need some more life insurance, you can say, 'I have all that I need.' 'Who told you?' 'John Savage.' Click!"

Next Year

Twelve months later, Dr. and Mrs. Doctor come to my office for their first annual review. I put a clean set of circles on the chalkboard.

"How much do you have in the bank?"

"John, you won't believe what happened last year . . . all we put in the bank was $200 a month. We only have $5,400 here."

"Don't feel bad. Life's a cinch by the inch, hard by the yard. You can't take fifteen years of sinning and eliminate them by one year of penitence.

"Your $200 went in here (point at Insurance circle). This has become the new Tin Can because you are never going to use this anymore (point at Tin Can circle). You know what, it pays better than zero . . . 1.8%, 1.9%, 2% . . . it's not much, but you know that you can see the value now . . . you've got $5,000 in there and you've only got $4,800 here (point at Bank circle). This is the one of immediacy. We must get this up. If we don't, this is good money too (point to Insurance Circle). We'll use this. We need the money for something and it's there to be used.

"We've decided that we are going to do it this year. What I would like to see you do is to put $300 here (point to Bank Circle) and I want to put $300 here (point to Insurance Circle).

26

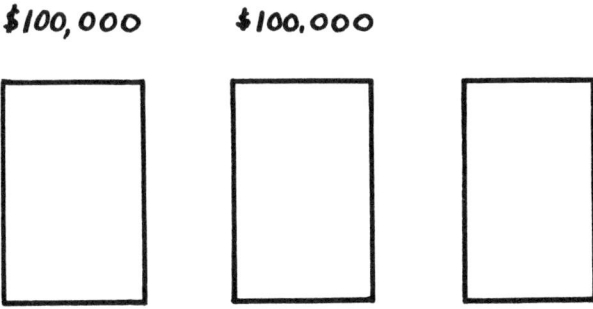

$100,000 $100,000

"Let me lay out your life insurance contracts in a more visable form for you. Here's the $100,000 that you had originally (point to the contract on the left); then you bought the second hundred (point to the contract in the middle) and these are two different companies you had before I came on the scene. Let me help you with both of these contracts as they are the best policies you will ever buy. As your program was moving along well, these get better and better.

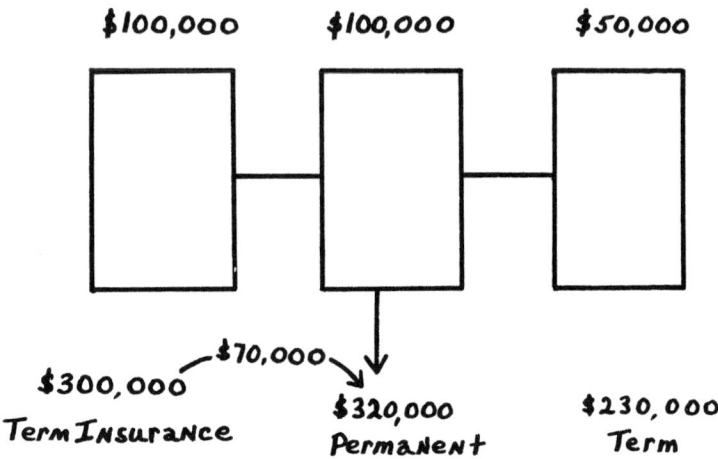

$100,000 $100,000 $50,000

$300,000   ─$70,000─

Term Insurance $320,000 $230,000

Permanent   Term

"They're called dividends. This happens to be $50,000 of ordinary life that you bought from me. We've put it in red because it is in the red. It's not worth much yet because it is in its embryo. My commission is paid out of that and that is why I don't charge you for my total financial services because I'm well paid in the form of commission. $300,000 more is down here which we call term insurance.

"It serves a purpose because it's affording the protection that we need. But let's examine this, the $250,000. It is pumping into this savings vehicle (point to the policies). The $300,000 will some day, but let's say for simplicity sake, this is the good stuff (point to the $250,000) and this is the bad stuff (point to the $300,000). It's not bad for protection but every dime we're putting in this direction we are putting down the drain at really an increasing rate because this is one-year term insurance.

"This year we want to convert $70,000 of the term so that we will have $320,000 of permanment and $230,000 of term. What

I'm leading up to, two years from now, is to convert another $100,000 of this; let's not do any thing this year. Next year you shouldn't do anything but I will be back and if you haven't done this I am going to kick you and I'll start taking the money to the bank for you. (If I convert at the end of the first year I must make a note in my files so that I don't even talk about converting the following year. When I do see him the following year I start off by reminding him that he isn't to convert anything this year.)

"The beauty of this is, remember that you're never going to buy any more life insurance, you have all of the life insurance you are ever going to own. After we convert this hundred, you'll never, ever pay any more in premiums and we'll convert the balance of the $130,000 two or three years down the line just from the dividends from all of the policies. You have only one more increase in premium payments coming along in the history of your program."

*   *   *

I use dividends to buy more insurance. I don't want to see dividends stay in the policy because they don't stay in mine. They shouldn't stay in my clients' contracts.

Chapter 4

BREAKFAST: THE MOST IMPORTANT MEAL OF YOUR DAY

Do you remember reading in your grade school health books about the importance of a good breakfast to get you started in the morning? I agree 1,000 per cent and it isn't because I own shares of Kellogg's and it's not because I'm into health foods. To me, breakfast is an ideal setting for meeting with a client.

First, I've found that almost everyone can meet you for breakfast as long as you're willing to get up early.

Best yet, you will be dealing with a clean slate. If you see someone before that person goes to work, before he's gotten some bad news, has had a raft of telephone calls, then you've caught him before he's had a chance to form a particular attitude about you, your "interruption," or the day with his own ups and downs.

Lunchtime is the worst time to call on a businessman. He'll have lunch with you, but you must understand that you are consuming about two of his most important hours. If you manage to get an appointment in the first place, it could easily be broken. Everyone sets priorities and if a prospect has anything else going, he'll probably cancel your date.

Breakfast is perfect. People aren't likely to cancel breakfast appointments because their business day doesn't really start until they arrive at work.

And by the way, it gets you going early, too. On days when I'm working hard, I like to schedule two breakfasts. I start when the prospect wants to meet.

To keep in shape, I also try to run or work out every day or every other day. When someone wants to see me at 8 a.m., I'll most likely run a few miles before I have that breakfast. If I see someone at 7 a.m., I may just have juice with the prospect and work out afterwards. If I have two breakfasts, I might have juice at one, a regular breakfast at the second and save the workout until the afternoon.

Most agents do not get up early enough to have breakfast appointments. But if you start the practice, you'll understand why I say this business is getting easier. I'll bet that I'll have 100 breakfasts in 1980, and have nothing but positive results. Oh, you can pay for the breakfast, too, and you won't go broke. You only go broke buying dinners and drinks.

The salesperson who thinks the prospective buyer has to be wined and dined simply does not understand the chemistry of mankind. That person is entertaining a myth.

Business that is bought by entertainment will be lost by entertainment because somebody can always out-do you. Give a guy a dinner, and the next guy gives him a television set, and so on.

I don't think you buy clients. People want to do business with someone they trust and someone they respect.

Also, I happen to believe if you stay out drinking and entertaining every night, there is a chance that you'll endanger the soundness of your marriage. For me this type of prospecting for business is just a dead-end on two counts.

Many people reading this book are going to disagree with me, but if two people agree on everything, one isn't needed.

My conclusion: Many people want to produce the way I do, but if they want to use other methods, they might be hurting themselves with some of them.

Chapter 5
PROSPECTING

When I entered this business, many agents used direct mail prospecting on the theory that 1,000 direct mail contacts would get 100 replies, and the 100 replies probably would produce 10 sales. Also, stamps cost 3 cents and there was a thing called a penny postcard.

Prospecting in the last five to ten years has undergone a radical change which is due to a more sophisticated buying public and a society that has become more service-oriented.

Cold calling, another popular prospecting method of the Fifties, is much less popular today. I thought it was dumb then, and I think it's more dumb now.

Joining organizations is another approach to prospecting. You could build short-term friendships which supposedly could vault you into a favorable selling interview.

Finally, personal friends and relatives are always seen as targets since, psychologically, they would have difficulty saying no to you.

Many of these methods are not professional and we're in an era when the buying public is demanding professionalism.

In my estimation the only reliable method of prospecting is to employ the referral system. I believe it's the only comfortable way to put the agent in front of the buyer.

There are two kinds of referral: one, the satisfied client calls an associate on your behalf and suggests that your services be retained; two, if one is too bold, the client opens the door by suggesting to the friend that we at least meet.

It's the only way I work. For example, back to my favorite meal. On his birthday I will take a client out for breakfast just for the chance to see him. I'll make it a point to tell him that we are *not* going to talk about his insurance program.

This relaxes him and about half-way through breakfast, I'll ask him if he's happy with me as his agent. Now, there's not a soul alive who, on his birthday, having breakfast with you, is going to say he's dissatisfied.

Then I ask if his wife ever refers her obstetrician or pediatrician to another person. The answer is always yes! That's it during breakfast.

Outside I lean against my car (I gave this hint to one young agent who said he leaned against the client's car and the client drove away) and I say something like this:

"You know, something is troubling me. You say that you are happy with me as your agent, then you say your wife recommends her doctors to her friends; but, you've never recommended me to anyone, and I wonder if there's a problem?"

The response is usually, "Hey, John! I can recommend you to a lot of people!"

And my reply is, "I don't want to be recommended to a lot of people . . . just one person, who you will call, and say that you think I'm a decent, pleasant fellow and you'd like us to have breakfast together and get to know each other."

I assure my client that I would never do anything to hurt our relationship or put him in a compromising position, a fact he knows about me anyway.

Approaching a person through a third party offers a much more favorable selling position than a direct approach.

By the time I pick up a telephone to call the new prospect, my client will have called him. I rarely, if ever, talk to anyone that hasn't been contacted in my behalf before I make the call.

Once the situation has been favorably established by my client, it's up to me to destroy it. I've got to be very bad if I can't follow through. I'll say something like this when I call:

"You don't know me from a bottle of Vicks, but Jack Major called you about me, and he thinks the two of us ought to get together. What I'd like to do is have breakfast with you to share a few ideas, and if I can be of help, fine. Do you have any objections to that?"

They almost always answer, "no", when you ask about objections. But most people would say no if you called them and said, "Hey, Jack Major told me to give you a call, can you come to my office and discuss what I'm about?"

I like to start out with a new prospect at breakfast because I also don't believe in doing business in anyone's home or in someone else's office.

I come unarmed, no briefcase, no bunch of papers! If a guy says he needs $100,000 of life insurance right now, I can't do it. I'm going to do something different, something that will ignite a spark in his chemistry that says, "I like what I'm seeing here."

Other methods of prospecting have become trite. You know how you react to a direct mailing. If you're a thinking person, you probably throw it away. Do you want non-thinking persons as clients? No! So it's axiomatic that you will not use direct mail.

I'm sure that people who promote direct mailings will not be very excited about this idea, but if you believe in something, you have an obligation to share it.

Cold calling will take you down the path of sales self-destruction, even though many teach it today and adhere to the technique.

Cold calling wastes time, it's psychologically defeating to the agent, and it has a false ring. The buyer knows that you're really not "just in the neighborhood."

If you see 20 people going door to door, and you get 20 "no's", that has to bother you. There is no mind equipped to take all those losses at one time without suffering detrimental effects.

I believe that a mind needs a lot of wins to function effectively and productively. Why not provide yourself with favorable conditions that get you in a comfortable position to sell?

I'm a tranquil person, and I'm certain it's because I spend so much time thinking about how to do things the easiest way. It's behavioral.

Your purpose is to accomplish as much as possible during the course of a day. You know that you're going to hear 20 rejections before you get one "yes" on a cold call day. You may get a person that just wants a friendly warm body in the house or office because the person is lonely and could use some conversation. That's not your purpose.

The life underwriter who thinks he works a full day every day is lying. I don't know if the average is three or four hours per day, but most people don't work all day. They procrastinate from the time the sun comes up until it goes down, and they do not attack their work.

Yet, they will call on a businessman who works a 12 or 14-hour day, and they don't understand, even then, that to excel in any field a person must work a lot of hours.

Few people excel! To be successful you have to be bright, industrious, and you have to have guts. It takes all three.

A big reason for lack of productivity is basic reluctance to make calls. It is not uncommon. It's built into the chemistry of just about everyone.

I spend a lot of time raising money for charitable purposes and people think I enjoy raising money. Not at all! So I do it, since someone must, as easily as I possibly can. You do that by calling on people who have a fair amount of money.

It's the Willie Sutton approach. Or like the priest who talked to the new couple in the parish after services, and they agreed to contribute $300 over three years to the church building fund. The next week, the couple's pledge for $3,000 over three years appears in the church bulletin. The couple goes to the priest and he is all apologies. "I'm really, really sorry about the mistake," he says. "I assure you I'll correct it in next week's bulletin."

Call reluctance is another way of saying you don't want to be turned down, and I don't know anyone who does. It's another reason making cold calls is so rough.

Joining clubs and organizations is antiquated and it's slow. If I've got to sell my friends, then my product probably isn't the best.

Lastly, if I have to rely on personal relationships before I can bring up the fact that I'm selling something meritorious, then I better look at what I'm selling.

Why put someone in an uncomfortable position? I have many friends that became friends by becoming clients, but it has been many years since I turned a friend into a client. I sold one neighbor; he approached me first.

I've been chairman of the University of Toledo board of trustees, and I have one TU client. I can't say I've used the position to enhance my business. I personally would be extremely uncomfortable turning associates into clients.

Let me qualify what I have said. There's nothing wrong with selling a few friends when you're starting your career. However, early on, you should begin to rely on referrals. Don't try to make 400 new friends so you can make 400 new sales.

Good Prospects

Every living, breathing human is a prospect but if I were to list the best sources, I'd say the small business owner, the physician, the accountant, the lawyer, and yes, the salesman.

The highest income in society will be found in this grouping, excluding presidents and a few top executives of major corporations. I don't include them because my chances of getting in front of them in a comfortable, favorable way are not very good.

Working in the major corporation executive market takes a lot of time, and I still prefer to work where I'm most comfortable. Also, after you get by the top slots of major corporations, you'll encounter lower income groups.

Example: General Motors may have a major plant in your community, headed by four executive vice-presidents, and 24 vice-presidents, all with incomes in excess of $50,000 a year. In the same community, there are probably 400 businesses with owners each making more than $50,000 annually.

The small corporate head is used to making decisions. Too often that major corporation's chief executive has to take the decision to a committee or board more often than not, whether it's a major purchase, stock purchase, pension plan, or whatever product you're trying to market.

It reminds me of those old strings of Christmas tree lights. You don't have lights unless all the bulbs are wired, and if one goes out, you're in the dark. It's a tough arena. Good results are difficult, and they are rare.

The small corporate leader, the successful sole proprietor, usually is an entrepreneur who does not go by the book. I find this type of person is unusually bright, a fast thinker, someone who shoots from the hip.

This person usually has good insights and a deep level of sensitivity. He or she communicates well and does things easier than the average person.

A warning: With the kind of insight this prospect usually has, make doggone sure you are prepared, otherwise, you'll be picked apart.

Also don't call on that person festooned with charts, tables, slide shows and a portable office. He wants it brief and to the point. He wants you to talk in short sentences.

A friend gave me that advice when I was 27. He said, "Talk to me in short sentences. Be concise! All I have is time, and the longer you're here, the more you're cutting into it."

SOLE PROPRIETOR: A sole proprietor probably is more interested in service and less interested in price than you might think. This type of client builds his own successes on quality and reliability, the kind of trust relationship that you want.

PHYSICIANS: Most of them have great integrity, are extremely busy, and know very little about business. In fact, to say they know anything about business would be a compliment. They're science-directed. They're looking for someone they can trust to handle the other business aspects of their lives.

A physician is a good prospect because he will refer you to other physicians, very often without you having to ask. I receive calls from physicians who have talked to one of my clients. There isn't any way to improve on that kind of referral.

If you don't sell that prospect, get out of the business. He came to you first.

I'm very comfortable with this group because I find people of high intellect who understand and appreciate knowledge of the product and your willingness to serve their needs.

ACCOUNTANTS: Fine prospects, and like the physician, they appreciate competence and will have an even greater referral base.

They are in the small business world and they know their small businessman needs some help. When you build a trust with an accountant, you know he will refer you to his clients.

And when you come in from the top side like that with an inside recommendation from someone's accountant, you're going to be in beautiful shape.

ATTORNEYS: They are good decision-makers, and they understand the importance of good estate planning. Most lawyers seem to associate with other lawyers, making it easier for you to attract them as clients if one attorney finds your work to be satisfactory.

Last, and not really last at all, salesmen are beautiful prospects. They are positive, they make decisions, and they usually have higher incomes. In fact, the successful salesperson, on the average, makes more money than any "average" representative of another field.

There are thousands of salespeople making more than $100,000 annually, and a person selling a service instead of a product earns more.

The radical change I've experienced over 29 years in the sale of life insurance is the explosion of service-oriented businesses, and the people in those fields are a rich resource for financial planning. A prime example is the owner-operator of a fast food unit or units and is someone who usually is in a high income bracket. His assistants or managers are paid well, and that creates another complete level for prospecting that so many persons overlook, even the agent selling the owner forgets that resource. When you are referred down the ladder, by the president, there's no possible way the person on the lower rung can refuse to see you.

I have 50 clients who are associated with McDonald's. I started by being referred to Bert Rose and Jerry Isan, the first McDonald's franchise holders in Toledo. When you think of the thousands of people employed in Toledo by the Golden Arches, I don't even scratch the surface.

There's a sub-category through all these prospects that I referred to in one of the selling ideas, the single person, man or woman.

The single career woman in fact may be the best prospect for a new person entering the business. You know, singles relate to singles, and young people relate to other young people.

We have great numbers of college graduates each year, they're the largest age bracket, and there are fewer life insurance agents today than there were 25 years ago.

Much like the corporate farmer, who farms more acreage than ever before, a smaller group of agents is doing more business. All of that makes it harder for the new person to survive long range, so singles become a great place to start. If you write 100 new policies, they will give you the base you need. We know the person who writes 100 new life insurance policies each year for five years probably will have 300 clients with that base of business. The better you serve your clients, the better they will serve you.

Remember, too, you always want to upgrade your clientele. The referral method of prospecting increases your chances for doing this as a good client will send you to another.

You don't want pot luck in client selection. Obviously, you want quality human beings which has nothing to do with income brackets. Build a quality clientele and it doesn't matter if the persons involved are mailmen, dentists, or whatever, that business is going to be substantial, and it will stay on the books.

By the way, selectiveness is a two-way street. When you have your eye on a particular prospect, or category of prospects, remember you're being watched as well.

I said it before, but it should be repeated. Today's buyer is sophisticated, expects you to have a certain amount of knowledge about your product, and expects integrity with service.

At the same time, your reputation with other persons will govern the reception you are or are not entitled to get from prospective clients.

Chapter 6
BUSINESS INSURANCE

Emerson said that any business is nothing more than the lengthened shadow of one man (or, I would like to add, one woman). If we agree with this, then there is no real reason for calling on a company board of directors or administrative officers. Instead, schedule a breakfast (or lunch appointment) with the individual who runs the company.

Most companies are run by one person. While there may be a collective group of advisors, my experience says that one figure is the overriding personality when a decision is made.

If I'm right, then I think it's a cardinal sin to have an appointment with more than one person. I did it to myself just this year. I found myself at breakfast with the president and vice-president of a company, and believe me, I didn't care for the situation. "Break-Fast" is about what it was, and with two against one, their chances of scoring were much better than mine. If you're in that two-on-one situation I think you will find yourself on the defense through most of an interview.

I've always believed that any family that has a closed corporation business should try to buy most of the life insurance coverage inside the corporation. The corporation is a powerful vehicle for handling a multiplicity of coverages and so relieving the individual from after-tax expenditures.

Let's talk about dealing with the small corporate owner, to let you know how I handle the sales situation from start to finish, and reactions you can expect.

As a general rule, the person I am talking about has two problems, he's the head of his family and the head of his business. The odds are, too, that the person is more wrapped-up in the business, spending far more time attending to the company than to the family.

(Allow me this personal departure, and take it for what it is. I tell everyone: No success in the field compensates for failure at home.)

I find many men are not giving any attention to their duties as a father, family head and partner in raising children. If you were to hit the businessman with that statement, immediately you would turn off 80 per cent of them. They'll say, "Who are you to tell me what to do and how to operate!"

I'd rather approach them as follows:

"Mr. Businessman, most people that meet with you talk about your business problems, and I think you're going to find this interview refreshing. You were referred to me by _____, a good friend of yours. As I said to him, I would just like to meet you, share some thoughts, and if nothing else happens, we'll enjoy our breakfast and part friends.

"I'm not interested at all with your group insurance at work, your pension plan, or profit sharing plan. Later on, if you like what I'm about, we're probably going to discuss many facets of your business to see if I have any solutions to some of your problems. But first I would like to talk about your personal situation."

Talk about his problems, not yours.

I ask if he has a new or old will . . . or no will. If he says he just drafted a will, I ask about a trust, and introduce the trust mechanism as a means of good estate planning.

This isn't a textbook, and I'm not going to get into explanations about a trust, but I advise anyone who hasn't already done so to look into it. I find that talking trust is probably the greatest catalytic agent for doing business with a business owner than any other vehicle at our disposal.

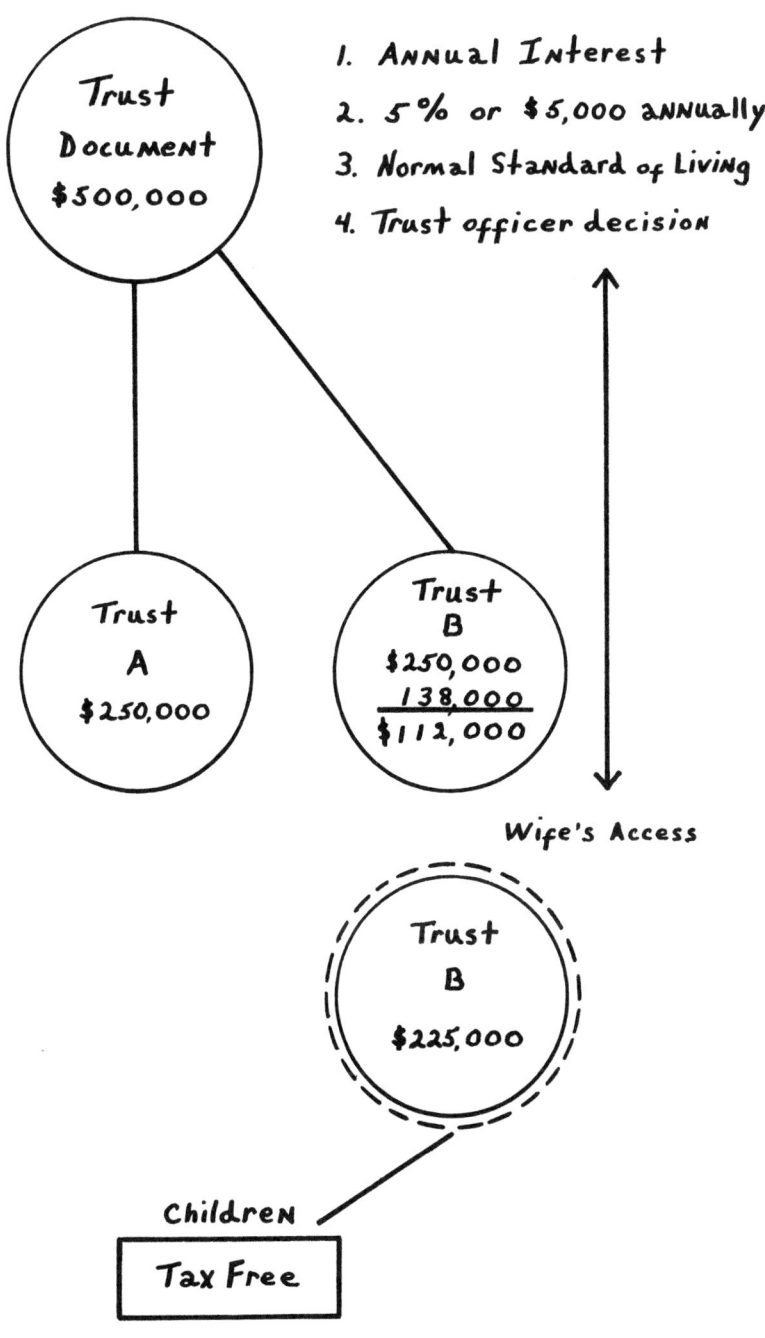

In selling the trust concept, I make statements like, "Why don't you take advantage of your bank's offer to have a trust implemented with no cost to you during your lifetime?"

Then I follow by drawing an illustration of a trust, the large circle. It represents a document drafted by a lawyer, and the only cost will be his charge of $300 or more, depending on the degree of sophistication required. It's called the A-B Trust.

A new will is drafted at the time with a pour-over provision so that most of the individual's assets ultimately end up in the trust.

I show them that at death, $250,000 goes into Trust A tax free because of marital deductions.

Trust B is $250,000 minus $138,000—the specific exemption that is given all estates.

So the result is $112,000 to be taxed, an amount of about $25,000.

Then I erase the B circle, and show $25,000 subtracted from $250,000, leaving a new circle of $225,000.

The beautiful thing is the wife has all of Trust A, and can invade Trust B for the annual interest, and 5% or $5,000 of the corpus each year, whichever is greater.

It also can be invaded for a normal standard of living, and finally, if a trust officer deems it necessary for the wife to have more money, it can be invaded again for that purpose.

The reason I bring that out is so the wife doesn't think she is handcuffed when it comes to invading Trust B. This explanation usually relaxes everyone.

But like the Wedding feast at Cana, I save the best until last.

I explain to the businessman that the beauty of the trust is when the second person dies. Then all of Trust B passes on to the children tax free. And it's the only vehicle known to man that makes that statement possible. In most instances, people say, "Hey! we ought to do it."

How does that sell life insurance, you might ask? In some instances, there is no need for additional life insurance, but I hope we don't put a price tag on doing a job for people.

In most cases, especially with larger estates, life insurance is needed to provide liquidity. And the more liquid a trust is, the more efficiently it will operate.

A trust minimizes taxation in estate planning, but more than that, it conserves and later distributes the estate if the owner dies at an early age.

Experience has taught me that most strong business people spend an awful lot of time with the business and really don't do the job needed in personal planning.

Worse, most of their wives do not involve themselves to any great measure in the business, or even in the major financial decisions of the family. Maybe this is because of the business-man's aggressiveness and an assumption by his wife that he is the end-all in finance; regardless of the reason, we know that too many important family planning decisions get side-stepped or ignored.

Most men don't have a trust. Secondly, every liquid dollar usually is used to promote business. Thus, they die leaving the business in bad shape and their family in poorer shape.

All their money is tied up in buildings, equipment and land, and when liquid dollars are needed to pay estate taxes, the beneficiary, the wife in most cases, is forced to sell assets to get money to pay the government. So the true estate value already starts to shrink since a forced sale brings fewer dollars.

You know this. You have to whet your customer's appetite, and you do that by convincing him of your real concern for helping. It probably does not involve talk of life insurance whatsoever in the first several interviews. It involves good planning.

I don't sell wills, and I don't sell trusts. But when we get into planning and my client sees that the work is done satisfactorily, there is no difficulty moving from personal matters to corporate matters.

I use power phrases like, "You've taken a lifetime to build your business. Why don't you take just a few days to plan for its distribution?"

"You've taken a lifetime to build your estate, doesn't it make sense to take a few days to decide how you're going to dispose of it?"

These are not original phrases, I know, but I've made it a part and parcel of every interview I have with a business person. If I know that a great amount of dollars are needed to cover a liquidity problem, I also know that it would be almost impossible for a businessman to own $200,000 or $300,000 of life insurance if it required a personal annual premium of $9,000 or $10,000.

Why? A businessman will write all kinds of checks, big checks at work. Yet, he's a totally different person when writing checks out of his personal account, even if he's written 50 small checks to the phone company, the bank, or the department stores. I sometimes say this:

"You know, this year you have written $2 million worth of checks for somebody else. Doesn't it make sense to write one for yourself?"

That's a power phrase. You say it in simple language and an individual understands.

Now that we've introduced the problem, we need a solution, and the solution is the size of the life insurance policy that requires a premium from someone.

The answer? Use your corporation dollars. It's far, far easier. It's before they're taxed. It should make a lot of sense and here's the idea as I have used it over the last five years.

"Mr. Worth, you have put all of your working years into developing this company, and now it truly depends on your leadership and guidance, even though you have 10 employees." (This is based on an interview with a man who had told me his Number Two man had been with him several years but was not yet capable of running the company.)

I told him I had an idea that I believed would fit perfectly into his situation since his family was pretty well grown, he was in his late fifties, and his wife was in her mid-fifties.

I turned to her and said, "Mrs. Worth, if your husband were to die, how long do you think it would take you to sell this business?"

If she could sell it at all, she said, it would take a long time because the business was built to a large degree around her husband's personality.

If that really was the case, I said, then she definitely would be interested in what I had to say.

Mr. Worth said his company was valued at $200,000 and I told him he should purchase $100,000 ordinary life insurance with a 10-year $100,000 level term rider.

"Then if something happens to you," I said, "your wife instantly has a buyer for the business ... The Columbus Mutual Life."

If Mrs. Worth is fortunate enough to sell the company, she gets a bonus. If there is insufficient coverage on her husband, and there is no ready buyer, she could literally give the business away, a situation that would certainly impair her living style for the next 10 years, and could bring sadder times in retirement.

The couple nodded their heads in agreement, saying since they were making good money at the time, they might as well insure the permanency of company assets.

* * *

If I had the guts, I would have asked for $200,000 ordinary life because I think it was needed; but I still have difficulty asking for so large a premium ... I can't get away from this feeling.

One of the biggest problems I have is that I always put myself in the other guy's position and picture myself writing his check. When it gets too big ... I don't want to write it either!

Mr. Worth was an individual referred to me. He told me during our first meeting that a close personal friend sold him all his present coverage, which totaled about $80,000. Later, I found out, that agent also was guardian of the Worth's children and their money, if he and his wife were killed in a common accident.

I comment on this because I can't imagine a more difficult selling situation. If I had been thinking clearly, I should have closed the interview when I first learned about the relationship and merely talked about something else.

Since that interview, the idea many times has been a tremendous help in closing sales involving sole proprietors. There are more new businesses starting all the time, and more often than not, they are being established by sole proprietors.

Everybody talks about planning, but few people plan their business activities. Often, many practitioners in our field make planning so complex that the person says, "Heck, I'm going to be so busy, that I don't have time to plan."

It's our duty to make ideas simple and to make our clients understand that the concepts are not complex. In every interview I try to minimize the amount of time the customer needs to set aside for our meetings.

Chapter 7
WHAT YOU SAY IS WHAT YOU GET

There are no video replays on a first impression. It's what it says it is.

What you say to a business owner, executive officer, or employee on a first meeting is critical since you're going to be studied from the moment you say, "Hello!"

We can talk about likely sales prospects and the selling ideas that might be of interest to them, but if the initial impression you give is not positive you'll never get to tell them the great ideas.

The worst mistake you can possibly make, in my opinion, is to talk about insurance. Possibly, insurance just may be the most uncomfortable word that your prospect could hear you utter.

The only equally uncomfortable situation I can think of is being a white man on a 100-yard dash starting block.

Don't be in a hurry. Most business cases that I write have an incubation period of three to six months and in about 50 per cent of the businesses I contact, the owner's business house is in much better order than his personal house.

Make sure, when you see that your prospect has done a great job of personal and business planning, that you compliment the achievement. It will strengthen your personal relationship, and also the relationship with your referrer.

Playing hard to get is an old idea, but one that sometimes doesn't hurt if you're sincere and you can carry off the move gracefully.

At this stage in my career, there is no one client who is going to dictate my future. I let this be known, and I think I do it nicely. Some personalities can handle a statement like this, and there are some who cannot.

Sure, I want more clients, and I truly enjoy working with them, but I don't want to have any more problems either. I've been through those times.

I give the client a litte background on me, how I got to see him, and I tell him I work very slow. This I emphasize.

"I may work too slow for you," I'll say. "I'm not in a hurry, and the sun will come up tomorrow." Sometimes I add: "There's not one thing you can do that will upgrade my income." (But don't say that if it isn't true!)

Stay at ease, and stay relaxed. Bringing lots of papers and pamphlets to the first interview is bound to hurt you. I have it in my brain, I have the experience.

I'll spend an hour or more with a person and we won't have conducted any business. We'll talk about some things, and all I say is, "Does this make sense to you? Does any of this make sense?"

The big thing is that he says "yes", which is when I say, "Why don't we set a time in the next few weeks where you can come to my office and we'll be able to talk about things a little more?"

I ask, in the meantime, if he has any reservations about giving me copies of a will, or trusts so I can have a notion or an idea ahead of time about what his additional plans might be.

I'll say, "Do you know of any reason why I can't look at your will?" and they say, "no."

All my appointments are in my office if at all possible so I can get to the drawing board.

People buy people, they don't buy insurance. And if they buy you, they'll do what you tell them. I didn't have a dozen interviews last year that failed to result in a sale.

There's another thing I now do in a business interview. Usually it's the other way around, but I give my prospect my financial statement. Why? I want him to know he's in the hands of someone with a track record in business and someone who has his own house in order, that he isn't talking with someone who is late on his house payment.

One of the ironies of life to me is that so many people are giving so much advice and not taking it at the same time.

I have no trouble building a trust with a business client. I know, for example, that a guy who owns a McDonald's franchise which is doing a million in annual sales will write a certain number of checks for a certain amount of money. How do I know? I've had that experience myself.

If he has three McDonald's doing three million I also know the individual is worth a lot of money. Since he can sell them for 50 or 60 cents on the dollar I know that the worth of these franchises is $1.5 million.

Trust begins to gel for a variety of reasons. Sometimes it's just because you're open with a client and he'll be open with you in return. He knows you can talk about a lot of things but you are not going to broadcast them all over the world.

If someone comes to me with a secret and says, "Here's something nobody else knows." My response, "Hey, don't tell me, and then just you will know. Then it'll be an even greater secret." I have a thing about secrets. I don't like them.

In my first interview with a businessman, I always say, "You don't know how many people in this community think you built your business from the ideas you got from your accountant."

He'll say, "Yeah. Isn't that dumb?" He knows and I know how a business is built. It's built by the person's ingenuity, aggressiveness, talent, skills, and so on.

Once he responds to me that way, never again will he direct me to talk with his accountant . . . or the attorney about his business. I will only go to them when we need their expertise in their own fields.

I've been on earth too long. I know there aren't teams in business. Many, many accountants don't understand the need for great amounts of life insurance. I personally have never met a wealthy accountant.

Now, how can someone who has never been in the game understand if an estate is worth $3 million? The businessman can understand, and as a businessman, I can relate to him.

I get involved with attorneys and accountants usually after a sale is made, but in the meantime, I may have given the businessman some creative and innovative ideas that they are not even aware of.

The attorney or accountant, if dragged into a first session, often will say something to justify their own existence, like, "He hasn't done his planning and isn't ready for this." Or, "I believe in term insurance; I don't believe in ordinary." And he may be saying that because it's best for him, but that may not be the case for his boss.

I stress that I can give them a degree of objectivity in my reviews. "I don't charge," I say. "You can afford my price."

I tell them I've been in and out of more than 30 companies that have nothing to do with the insurance business so I've been there and have the experience to pass along.

56

Chapter 8
THE BUY-SELL AGREEMENT
(Or, How to Build Your Own Bank)

This idea is great for two businessmen who are co-owners of a corporation.

For simplicity sake, let's say each person owns 50 per cent of the business, valued at $300,000. They understand that their business will grow, but right now, that $300,000 is the company's true value.

I ask them: "How would you like $600,000? What if I could give you an idea that would insure each of you for $300,000? The premium would be deductible by the corporation, and it would be tax free to you. And one last feature, you can build your own bank."

You could get an answer like, "Boy, my accountant says we can't do that."

"Well", I say, "I think that something can be done, and the accountant will understand after I go through my procedure.

Let's say the premium for both totals $6,000, payable by the corporation. The premium is deductible if Partner B owns the policy on Partner A and Partner A owns the policy on Partner B.

The corporation owns both premiums at $3,000 each, so the partners can deduct the amount because it will be included in their income tax reports. In effect, they were given a $3,000 raise by the corporation.

The tax-free part? The dividend is a tax-free increment. The dividend here is 30 per cent of premium average over the lifetime. The corporation partners pay the government the taxes on the premium, but then the equivalent is returned via the dividend, making the package tax-free to the individual."

57

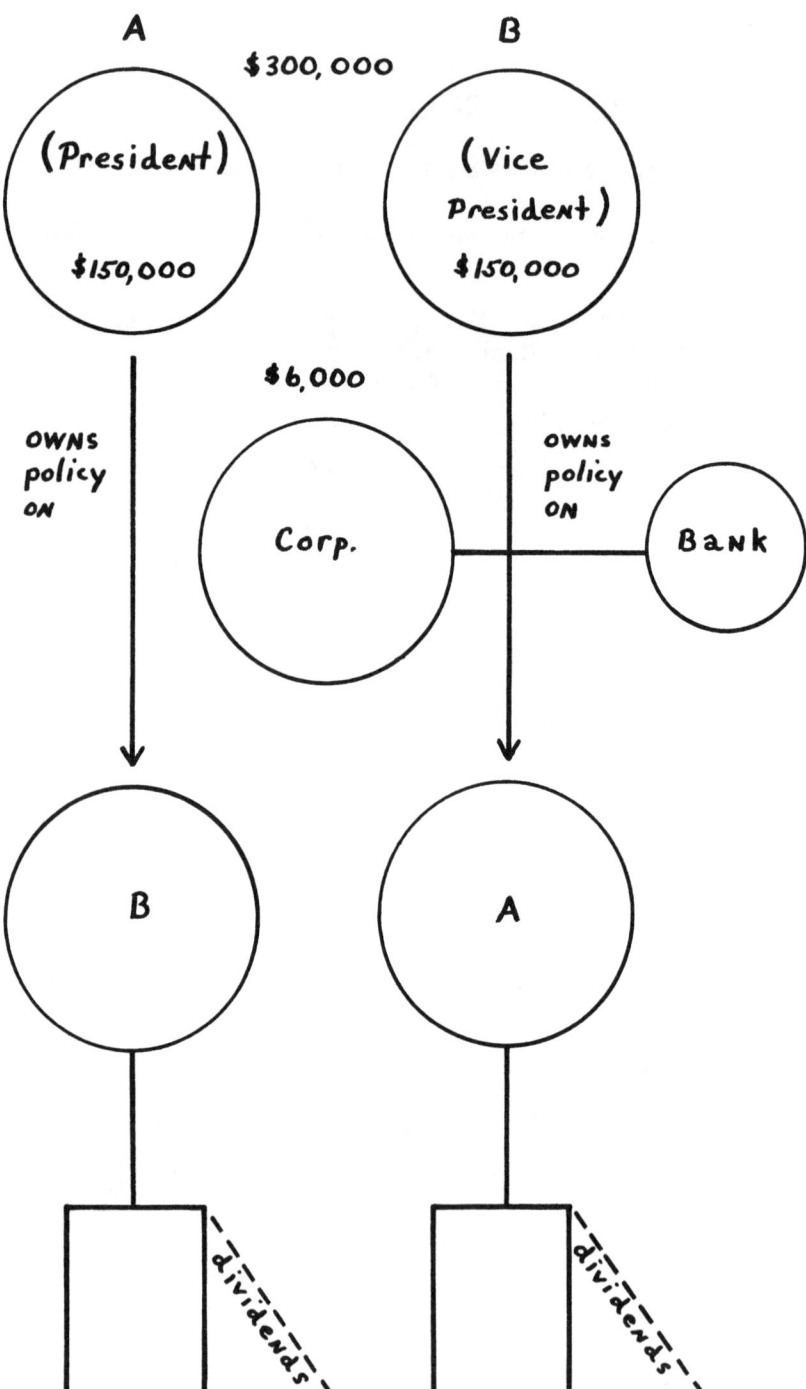

"I also said build your own bank and I mean it. You see, usually when your company needs a truck and it costs $25,000, you go to the bank and pay 10 to 12 per cent for the money. I'm saying that five years from now, when the firm wants a truck, you should buy it from yourselves. Each partner can take a loan from the policy cash values and present it to the corporation at 6 per cent simple interest.

"It's the interest our company charges on cash value, so you build your own bank for future use of the money.

"You see, chances are you're not going to die, soon. So we should talk about the living benefits of having the partners aid the corporation. Use the policies for their loan capabilities and you'll make 6 per cent, or whatever you decide upon, every time you transact a loan."

In layman's terms, it works like this:

A guy raises cats to sell the fur. It costs him too much to feed the cats, so he decides to raise some rats. He fed the rats to the cats, the cats grew up, he killed the cats, and sold the fur.

But he had a problem—the dead cats. He fed them to the rats. So he fed the rats to the cats, the cats to the rats, and the fur was free. If you can make it that simple, you're going to move a lot of business insurance.

Another Buy-Out

Here's a corporation where the book value on each of two partners is $100,000. I approached one of the partners and said, "Would you sell your part of the business for $100,000?" Answer, "no!" "How about $300,000?" "No." "A half-million?" "Well, I might."

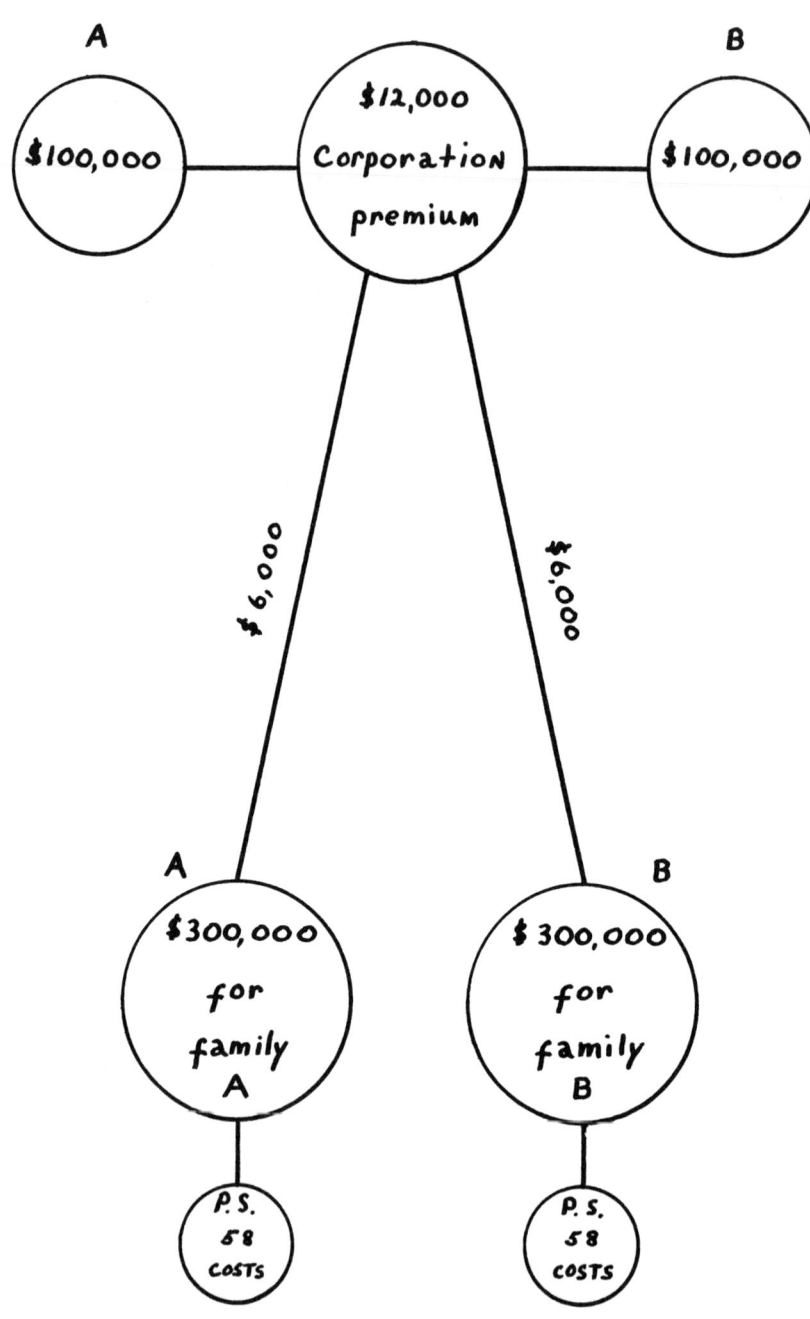

So, I arrived at a figure of about $400,000 and suggested this:

"You have your business agreement funded right now for $100,000. It's a redemption agreement. I don't want to bother that. But both of you knów that your wives and families are not going to be compensated properly if one of you dies and the family gets $100,000 for your stock.

"The business agreement, which is about nine years old, is antiquated. I'm not saying upgrade the agreement, although that's really what I would do, too. First, however, make sure your family gets $400,000 for your share of the business.

"It's simple. Take out an additional $300,000 in ordinary life insurance, and make a split-dollar arrangement with the corporation. Use the corporation as the vehicle to pay the total premium. Employer pays all split-dollar. You pay the P.S. 58 costs,* so you are buying the coverage, in effect, for one-half of what term insurance costs you.

"The corporation will make sure it's going to get its money back, through what I use as a collateral assignment (assigning the cash values back to the corporation so it gets its portion if death should occur).

"Use the fifth dividend option so there will be life insurance purchased by the dividend to make up the cash value that has to be paid to the corporation. What you're doing is making sure your family gets the $400,000 that you believe is the value of your share, and it is not going to increase the value of the corporation if you do die."

It's simple, and another great idea for selling business insurance.

*Value of economic benefit to the "employee" is calculated by the use of the government's one-year term rates (P.S. 58).

Chapter 9
MOTION VERSUS DIRECTION

"Busy" is one of those great sounding words that say or sound like their meaning. To me, it means being occupied, creating a lot of motion but not necessarily going anywhere, like the worker bee.

How often have you watched a person working so feverishly that you were certain he was really accomplishing something, only to find out the opposite?

If one is to develop a success pattern, one must, out of all that motion, seek some degree of direction. It doesn't matter what an observer sees. What matters is what actually is happening.

I'm sure that many diligently working people believe they are making headway when all they are doing is acting out man and woman in motion. That's not to say motion isn't sometimes its own reward. I think it is. Often it's good, psychologically, to move for movement's sake. The jogger can go out and run and run and run to relieve anxiety. The miler, on the other hand, knows he has to fit a strategy to that motion to win the race.

Refusal to study oneself and weigh and evaluate carefully can, in many instances, compound problems. It has been stated that an unexamined life truly is not worth living. I think that's true, but even more so I think, is that the examination should occur on a daily basis.

No one can dictate a direction for you if you are in the sales field. Suggestions can be offered, but the salesperson must feel comfortable with the suggestion or it will not work.

In the life insurance industry we have a lot of agents who are all motion and no direction—all gears and no levers. They will spend endless hours shuffling papers in their offices, making neat stacks, writing lists, compiling numbers, all with no definable direction. The result of this is failure.

Wasting time is the disease of the salesman. Not all contract the disease, but the incidence is high.

Many trainers in the industry prescribe a certain number of calls, so many interviews, and a certain number of sales. This, too often, can just be accelerated motion which can end up as an exercise in futility.

I think teachers in this business should be discussing the quality of time, and should recognize that methods traditionally taught should be revised drastically if results are to be achieved.

We must also recognize that direction comes from two sources—from without and from within. I'd rather talk about the within, because no one seems to spend any time in this area.

God has given us much as human beings, and so often our talents and abilities go unexplored. Reflecting each day on what we are about will bring forth that inner direction. Once we understand ourselves and what we are, our minds can then tell us the best way to proceed. If any degree of direction is going to be achieved, I think it has to start out this way.

As for outer sources, outer direction must come from a good environment with good teaching. And that's not easy for a young agent to find.

Great trainers in our industry are scarce. If you happen to be associated with one of them, consider yourself very fortunate because you have an advantage over so many individuals who never have had the opportunity of good, basic, concentrated tutoring.

Call Reluctance

Call reluctance is one of those fears that may never be eradicated, but it can be mitigated with a little evaluation and good reasoning. What do I mean?

We must be comfortable about our way of life . . . personally comfortable. As adversity can introduce you to virtue, so can desperation bring you to tranquility.

In your first interview with a prospect, you will likely experience a measurable degree of uneasiness. But this will change if you are successfull in obtaining subsequent interviews.

On the other hand, if a person is discourteous to you initially, even if further meetings result from your first session, you probably will be uncomfortable. And a series of such meetings may find you knocking at the door of despair.

If this is the case, you must change your approach, and if you still are uncomfortable, then you should consider leaving the field of selling.

I doubt that you will come to that conclusion if you're honest with yourself. Let's face it, you've been hired by your company and you've passed a series of tests and interviews before you started selling, so obviously you are not devoid of some sales talent.

What does not surface, unfortunately, in the testing and talking stages, is the degree of fear you may have. I am persuaded that all of us have apprehensions to some degree. Okay, we agree that all of us have them, now what do we do about them?

First, we discount the myth that most prospects will turn us down.

Many supervisors tell their agents that if a prospect turns them down, they're really turning down the product, or the company, and not the seller.

I totally disagree. This may be tough to swallow, but I believe wholeheartedly that when a prospect turns you down he is turning *you* down. He didn't like you for some reason, and if the reason persists, you will fail unless you change.

You must become a likeable person to most people. Easily said, right?

It's not as hard as it sounds. If you conduct yourself in a manner that's agreeable to you, you'll feel comfortable with yourself. Once you truly are comfortable, you cannot imagine the sympathetic response of agreeability that you will notice in your environment.

Never go into an interview with the notion that you must make a sale. Enter with the idea that you must make a friend.

If we try too hard to sell a product, the buyer will be the first to know. Then the wall will go up, the defense mechanisms will spring out, and before you know it, you—and probably your customer—are ill at ease.

The outcome can be devastating.

There are probably no more than a half-dozen things you might be doing wrong, but unfortunately, they repeat themselves as innocently and earnestly as if they never happened before. It doesn't have to be that way. Remember, selling is an art, and artistic growth is a refining process.

Maybe we should call it the refinement of the truth.

Chapter 10

UNDERSTANDING

Understanding others probably is the greatest asset you can possess in trying to reach any degree of success in sales or any other field.

I'm sure much of the art is a gift from God, but I believe, too, that much can be learned. How, though, does one learn the art of understanding?

An intensive study of other human beings is needed. I have made this a lifetime commitment.

Early in my career, when I was building an agency and training young men and women, I constantly stressed the importance of studying the individuals they were to meet. I told them their clientele would come from all walks of life and from every sociological climate, just as my clients did.

In building an organization, I did not look for children of rich people, or children of well-known professionals. I looked for quality individuals willing to put in the time necessary to achieve a degree of success.

I must admit I did find a common denominator among all agents that I selected and had the privilege of working with during those years; they were good people. I believe if we're honest, and seriously think about it, we will conclude that most people will be good if you let them.

Let's talk about "in depth." There was a person who sold 30,000 drills in one location over a five-year period. Most people figured that 30,000 buyers wanted drills. Not so. They wanted holes.

That's what I'm talking about. Let's not be so myopic that we do not look farther and deeper when trying to get a better understanding of our fellow man.

All the people I've trained or had the pleasure of working with, had unique personalities. They had their share of bad days, days when they felt depressed. Sometimes the days turned into weeks.

I have often found this with agents who were trying to learn, and sell, and make house payments at the same time. That's a big order!

I learned that most of these people who were depressed for longer periods of time did not have a good opinion of themselves. I worked to help them know and love themselves.

It's tough to like yourself, however, if you have been dwelling for years in a sea of personal shortcomings. We all have weaknesses, and we all have strengths. Let's face it, God didn't make any perfect people, and I might add, I haven't met one yet who's even close.

I've told my trainees that each negative thought is a down payment on an obligation to fail. Let's try to understand the imperfect but complex human being. Let's look for the good points first and overlook shortcomings.

Remember my definition of a friend? It's someone who knows you very well and likes you anyway.

Think of some person you dislike and write down all the things you don't like about him. You might find it hard to get past five or six points.

That's not bad, is it?

What you've told yourself is that you really don't know that person, and maybe you should take a little more time to find out why the individual appears so unpleasant to you.

Maybe it would be ideal if all of us could capture a mother's love for her children. We've all heard about the mother of a convicted slayer, who when you ask her, says her child really isn't so bad.

It might be next to impossible to acquire that attitude, but we ought to get a little closer to others.

Your efforts to love and understand others will often result in unexpected openness from them, and a lot more insight for you.

Someone once said that we are three people; what others think we are, what we want others to think we are, and what we are.

I don't believe any of us can say all three of these personalities in us are the same, but we could try to get them closer. And we could make it a lifetime challenge to fuse them as much as possible.

The Greek philosophers said when they broke down the intelligence levels of a human being there are five grades: memory, command of mathematics and ratios, prudence, wisdom, and understanding.

They point out that a person can have a terrific memory and still be low on intelligence. The same is true about a person who excels at mathematics. Prudence? It requires an above-average intellect, and surely the men of wisdom have intelligence.

But Plato, Aristotle, and their contemporaries agreed that understanding is the ultimate level of intellect. They also agreed there was a point beyond which no man could go—understanding God and the creation of man.

If we all agree that the greatest living being is a human being, why don't we try to understand people?

Intelligence Ain't Education

On many platforms across the country, I've said that intelligence is an important ingredient for success in selling. But I should add that I think of intelligence and ability as tandem qualities, not interchangeable ones.

Intelligence is quick to comprehend. Ability is the capacity to act wisely on what is apprehended.

Intelligence is often used as a simile for education, and that's an error. It is probably safe to say that all Ph.D.s have above-average intelligence, but to assume that all are extremely intelligent would be incorrect.

I have spent nine years as a university trustee, and I'm positive that, collectively, its members are not among the most brilliant in our society.

In business, I find every successful entrepreneur seems to be gifted intellectually, and has great ability.

One thing that sets the Ph.D. apart from the person in the marketplace is discipline. Discipline, I would think, adds more to academic accomplishments than ability.

The person in the marketplace with any notches of success probably has an awful lot of ability, is extremely bright, and often has very little discipline. He gets by with brilliance and his ability to communicate.

Evaluate the sales person with that package in mind. He often has much innate intelligence, lots of ability, and communicates well. But lack of discipline can spin him into a mediocre level of productivity.

It's the guy we all know who does just what he has to and you probably would find that he didn't excel in the classroom for just that reason. If he graduated, he probably was a C student.

All of which brings me to the conclusion that the Ph.D. and the good salesman could learn something from each other; but since this isn't a book for Ph.D.s, let's look at what the salesman can learn.

I believe that challenge is one of the greatest aids to selling, and I challenge every salesperson now to read as many books as possible.

Start with one book. Statistics will show you that most people over 25 years of age never read books. See if you can read one book on *any* thing. Reading it will provide some additions to your vocabulary, and no one can have a vocabulary that is too broad. You can *use* too much of it trying to communicate, but you can't have too much command of the language.

During my travels I hear people say, "I can't become a CLU because I did so poorly in school." It's a more common statement than you would imagine.

What you did in school has absolutely nothing to do with what you're doing now. Accept the fact that you didn't read or study, or that you were a poor student with a crummy attention span. Then start today with a new educational process—educating yourself.

The message I'm passing on is, "Don't put yourself down. Give yourself a second, third, or fourth chance."

Read what you want to read first, then move to a subject that may be foreign to you. Better to begin reading a chapter at a time. Then tackle the whole book. If you say you're going to read a book, and you fall asleep after one chapter, you'll fall back into the same patterns and lose interest if you don't keep trying.

If you say you're going to read a chapter 20 pages long, then I think you should start disciplining yourself to reading that 20 pages with concentration.

What does all of this have to do with our business? To be successful, you have to be knowledgeable, and to be knowledgeable, you have to read. I personally feel that you'll get more out of reading than listening to tapes, although I don't discount the motivation factor that comes from listening to tapes.

It's kind of like the difference between driving and being a passenger. If I drive, I have to do the work, but I can ride and let my mind wander.

There are 1,500 pages in the new tax law. Rather than say you're going to read all 1,500 pages it would be good to take a short passage of five to ten pages, concentrate on them deeply and capture everything it has to offer.

Be the only life underwriter in your community who knows that part of the law thoroughly. Confidence, and a fire to learn more, will follow.

The learning process is like life itself. A cinch by the inch, hard by the yard.

There are university professors, hopefully not the majority of them, who quit learning once they attained their educational goal, and a degenerative process set in.

The same thing happens with a CLU or a Life Member of the Million Dollar Round Table. If that's your goal, I think you've short-changed yourself.

In the next 20 years, knowledge is going to take on a more pressing role because the buying public is demanding more competence.

At this juncture you may be saying that I've contradicted myself in *The Easy Sale*, and in the early pages of this book. I state that, in selling, knowledge of the product is not worth more than 5 per cent, and knowledge of people is worth 95 per cent. I haven't changed my thinking but the 5 per cent is important, and increasingly so. The catch is you should know 100 per cent of the 5 per cent.

My point is that discipline in understanding subject matter is a good starter for developing discipline in a more complex area—understanding people.

By the way, I'm not putting down education. It's a critical factor in the ultimate accomplishments of any person. But there are many, many ways to become educated, and just because tradition supports one way doesn't mean there aren't other methods.

Pursue your education, and encourage it for your children because it will give them certain advantages in life. But don't cry over spilt milk of 20 years ago because you can't go back and change things.

You can start a new life tomorrow, and you will be amazed at how little time it takes before you catch up with those who excelled in their younger years and failed to continue that discipline and educational process.

A word of caution: Don't fall into the trap, once you get into an in-depth study of the business, of trying to educate the buying public the same way. Take all that you've learned and simplify it so the knowledge is transmitted in a way people will understand.

You're not training your client. Build a trust with him or her. It's all we have. Once it is there, you are the only one who can destroy it.

Chapter 11
WIFE TIME

Here's a question that you might believe is irrelevant to what we have been discussing. "Is your marriage developing as well as your business?"

If the answer is "no" then I suggest you take time to read this chapter carefully.

As I travel across the country giving talks, one question comes at me more than all others. "John, how do you have such a great marriage?"

There are about 650,000 people in various parts of the world that know I have a terrific marriage because I talk about it a lot and because I think it's important. So I'm not surprised when people ask me about my personal life.

It has happened more often than I can recall that a person tells me for 20 minutes, after asking me how to make his marriage better, that he is miserable, has the worst situation in the world and how his home life is deplorable.

Have you ever heard anyone say, "I'd just like to have the right partner"?

Try this one on. How about being the right partner? To answer all those questions, I think it's essential to know who that person is looking back at you in the mirror every day.

As a husband, a father, and a male, I'll tell you how I approach the subject.

First, when I made a commitment to get married, it was a lifetime commitment. I'll never forget the prayer I made on the altar during the mass that married my wife and me.

I said, "Dear God, I want to have the finest marriage that ever has been put together on the face of the earth, and I vow to work diligently that this may be accomplished, but I cannot do it without your help."

That was just a short prayer, but 19 years later, I can truthfully say I enjoy a beautiful, vibrant marriage.

You can start by telling your wife every day that you love her. If you're the guy who gets up every morning grumbling, wobbling your way into the bathroom, mad at the world, not too thrilled at the face looking back at you, moaning and groaning about daily duties, not saying hello, criticizing the cold eggs, slamming the door behind you—listen.

I'll tell you that the same person, if he gets up happy to be alive, whistling in the shower, saying hello with a smile, and complimenting his wife on the great breakfast—if he does that every day for six months, six months later he won't be lying about the breakfast.

The point is that you must create a beautiful environment in your home, and that starts with the relationship you have with your wife.

Compliment her regularly. It takes no skill to criticize, and I find that if you take care of the problems belonging to the face in the mirror, that's a full-time job.

Take time to have lunch with your wife occasionally. Maybe a weekend or two each year take her away, out of the home environment, especially if there are a lot of children at home.

If you are working every day, every evening, and Saturdays and Sundays, and you wonder why your relationship at home is degenerating, please make an adjustment immediately.

Remember, no success in the field compensates for failure at home. You may be the type of person who spends every free moment with one of your children, ignoring the partner who made it all work from the beginning.

I call it wife time. If you are willing to carve out three or four hours a week, to sit and talk with your partner, you will soon find that you have a more warm and beautiful home life.

Some of you may go week after week without sharing an inward thought with your wife, and she may be doing the same. I think that's unhealthy, and the end result will be disasterous.

I plan that every Friday, excluding some rare happening, I am going to have dinner, alone, with my wife. That started when we were first married, when we cooked hamburgers on the grill after the children had gone to bed.

Later we would go out one night a week for dinner. As the children got older, involved in basketball, weekend activities and so on, it has really ended up with the two of us having a sandwich at 11 o'clock at night.

But the fact remains that you need time together and away from everyone else to keep your relationship strong and growing.

I have told many audiences that if you are running around on your wife, you are a fraud. If you disagree with me, I'll be glad to debate it with you on one of your local television stations.

I was single until I was 29, had all my fun and excitement, and did almost everything I wanted to. Once I got married I said, "Now it's time to commit yourself to a permanent way of life that does not include stopping off at the bar, playing poker with the fellas, and other things so many people seem to need." I find my wife the most enjoyable entertainment in Toledo, just being with her.

I've heard many people say their husband or wife is not the same person they married. I think that's true of us all. You and I have changed a lot, if we take the time to examine ourselves. But I think if we take the position that we love and accept our mates for who they are, then we truly will not see their faults. Remember, they are putting up with a lot when they contend with us.

I believe all of you with families would agree that you would like to see your children have happy marriages, and if they cannot find an example in their homes, it's going to be difficult for them to accomplish that.

I believe a disciplined person is a happy person.

Lastly, continue to ask God's help. Keep your relationships strong with your maker and I think you will enjoy a fruitful life. Your attitude will dictate the results, but I think the attitude needs God as a complement.

Remember, if the channel is low on water, it is not the fault of the stream, but of the source. If your marriage is rocky, decide that it is totally your fault. Honestly.

If you accept 100 per cent of the responsibility and pray and work diligently to make things better, they will be better. Honest effort is always rewarded.

Three days before I was married, I took a Catholic priest to dinner and asked him for some words of advice on how to have a good marriage. His answer was succinct.

"Give in to your wife 100 per cent of the time."

I bought it and I'll pass it on to you. It works.

Chapter 12
HOW GOOD IS A GOAL?

No good at all, if no one shows you what is needed to achieve that goal. I think there's a gap in agency management. I don't care if the goal is $10,000, $5,000 or $2,000 and premium for a month for $10 million, $5 million or $2 million in production. There are a few important steps in reaching any goal.

Let's first try and understand the psychology of setting goals.

Everyone likes a winner and everyone likes to be one. If in fact anyone is going to be psychologically sound during a lifetime of selling, that person needs a series of wins.

We all get "no" a certain number of times, and we need a greater number of "yes's" if we are going to function effectively.

Probably none of us has more than two or three big events in a year that completely absorb us, but we all want and need them to be successful, whether it is planning the annual meeting or speaking at the Million Dollar Round Table.

If the events do not go over well, they are losses that really can be depressing.

One of the major measuring points of your year in the life insurance business probably will be the production goal you have set for yourself. Achieving it is a must. You know what kind of money you need to meet your bills, and what additional money you'd like to obtain over and above your basic needs. Your production and premium goals are targeted to that end.

But what about setting an upper goal and a lower goal as well—upper for what you want, lower for what you need. After you're in the business seven or eight years, you probably will need only an upper goal.

My goal for the last two years as been $20 million. Last November, I became painfully aware that $20 million was not going to happen, so I lowered my goal.

I achieved my second goal—a win—offsetting the first failure.

Map out a plan. Let us say that you must do $25,000 of premium to accomplish your goal. I contend that you have got to have a big January, and by that I do not mean $2,000 of premium.

You should not settle for anything short of $4,000 in premium for January, and $5,000 would be a lot better. Now comes the rub. How do you hit that goal?

You must label your January as an all-out month, meaning you are going to work night and day, and a half-day on Saturday if necessary.

Many audiences have heard me say that if you live in the northern United States, you might as well work in January because the weather is so miserable there's nothing else to do.

Don't let play get in your way. January is a prime work month.

Second, and this is important if you have been in business more than two years, your all-out month must include talking to your previous policy holders. You should devote November and December to setting up January appointments. Bring those people up-to-date on their programs and attempt to convert the term insurance that should have been put on as a rider in the initial sale.

Third, see friends whom you've been reluctant to call before. Remember, this is an all-out month, no holds barred. Do a few things that you aren't totally comfortable in doing. It's only for a month.

Finally, don't let a day go without asking at least one person to buy life insurance. Before you know it, you'll get to the point where you're asking nine people a day instead of one.

Follow these guidelines, and I'll bet you'll be amazed at your January. You'll also find that the $5,000 of premium will come easily. Once that premium goal is reached, you can't miss your $24,000 goal for the year because you are 20 per cent of the way there, and you've used only one-twelfth of the year.

Your January activity automatically will spill over into February, and you may find yourself doing an added $3,500 or $4,000 of premium that month. Given that, you will find yourself with $8,000 of premium at the least, procurred in the first two months of the year.

The biggest lesson you should learn from this program is that you will always be able to make a living (at this or any other business) if you get organized and work. And in our business, work means putting yourself in front of a prospective buyer at least once a day, in a selling interview.

Can you imagine working in any other industry and talking to only one person a day about your product? You'd be fired, unless you are selling 747's.

Understand that you are working against some negatives ingrained in this industry. Your industry has complimented the one-sale-per-week aim for years. Ignore that, and ignore company rules if they are the same, because it's only a compliment to mediocrity, and you do not enter this business to be mediocre. Remember, you have to satisfy the person in the mirror.

At the end of six months, if you have reached $17,000 of premium, take two weeks off. I have a saying that if you work hard, rest will be victorious.

If you have $18,000 of premium, take three weeks off, and if you have $20,000, take a month.

I cannot stress this philosophy too strongly because I believe the reward formula is essential for every goal-setting situation.

You owe it to your family, and to yourself, to take time off, and you will most assuredly function more effectively if you do.

So here comes October 1, and you are only 20 or 30 days away from your annual goal. Don't overreach it. I'll say that over and over again. Once you've hit $24,000, start thinking of the next year. Because *YOU HAVE MADE IT!*

Then repeat the process. By November 15 each year you want to begin organizing for the new year.

Take out a legal pad and start listing the people who are going to buy in January. It will become your super month, like it is for me. I write down as many as 100 names and while I may not sell them all, I'm sure I will sell 50 lives that month.

That's another thing we must address. Let's get 150, 200, 250 or 300 lives each year. Too many people are deeming themselves successful selling 30, 40, or 50 lives a year. In my opinion they are not doing a social justice to society. If they are capable, they should spread their talents to more people.

Every successful person in the life insurance business is goal-oriented. But remember this, too. You don't hear about the statistics for people who have set goals, failed, and because of the frustration, have quit the business.

Nobody likes to talk about the many who have been destroyed by setting goals that are unreal. If you understand your abilities and have a good look at your inner self, you won't do that.

We are people with different talents, and different gifts. Be assured that every company needs someone to place 5th, 10th, 50th, and 100th, as much as they need a first place finisher.

Only one person in your company will finish first. And I often find as I speak with home office conventions, the Number 20, Number 50, and Number 100 persons are among the happiest at the meeting.

Set your own goal, because no one else can. And master it. Don't let the goal master you.

Please remember that wisdom, strength, sensitivity, courage, and humility are not automatically bestowed upon you when you become 30.

Your maturity will be defined to the extent that those traits are cultivated and nurtured.

Narrowness, rigidity, and stubbornness all are signs of immaturity. Openness and flexibility will come with growing. They are the qualities that will flower with some effort.

Remember lasting power. That's why it's been easier for me. I have lasted, and God has given me the years to accomplish some of my goals.

And please remember, never tell yourself or others, "I've done my best," because no one ever has.

Selling Ideas

Something old . . . that has worked . . . and still does!

Something new . . . that's working . . . for millions!

Nothing blue . . . if you'll put them to work for you!

Ideas

#1 For The Single Young Man
"How Much? What Kind? When? From Whom?"

#2 Family Situation
"Economic Circle of Life"

#3 "For the Single Young Man Who Doesn't Need Insurance"
Situation A

#4 "For the Single Young Man Who Doesn't Need Insurance"
Situation B

#5 Decreasing Term Mortgage Insurance
The Wrong Product to Sell

#6 For The Successful Person

#7 "The Procrastinator"

#8 For The Recently Married Young Couple

#9 Estate Planning With The Family

Potpourri

Idea #1
For The Single Young Man
"How Much? What Kind? When? From Whom?"

I got the original idea for this presentation from another insurance company. It took them forty-two minutes; it takes me six.

(By the way, don't get confused with all the quotation marks you'll see throughout each presentation. They're all mine. As you know, I do practically all the talking in my sales interviews.)

O.K. I have the young man in my office, and I write the four questions in the above title on the blackboard. (See the illustration.)

Then I say to the prospect, "Young man, there are only four questions you have to answer:

"How much life insurance should you buy?

"What kind should you buy?

"When should you buy it?

"And from whom?"

(I point to each question as I give it. And I refer the prospect to each one again when I repeat them later.)

I continue, "I want to talk about these in the order of their importance to you; so first of all, how much should you buy?"

The young man doesn't usually come up with the right answer, but I do. And listen to the answer I give him. "An amount that you can easily afford."

IDEA #1

HOW MUCH?
WHAT KIND?
WHEN?
FROM WHOM?

Figure 1

Figure 2

TERM   ENDOWMENT

Figure 3

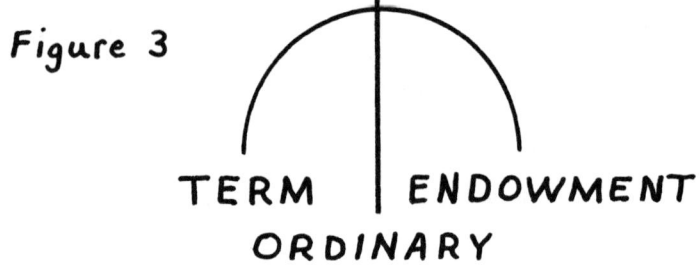

TERM | ENDOWMENT
ORDINARY

Nobody else is going to tell him that. In this business, you have to be different.

Then I ask him the second question, "What kind should you buy?"

Again I answer it for him, and I do it with the aid of a very simple illustration.

I draw a half circle (Figure 1) and say, "Young man, I want you to let this represent the entire scope of life insurance. At this end (Fig. 2) we put term insurance. At *this* end (Fig. 2) we put endowment. And up the middle, (Fig. 3) ordinary life."

(I write the words as I'm saying them. Then I point to them when I mention them again.)

"If I knew you were going to die tomorrow," I tell him, "I'd say to load up on term.

"If I knew you were going to live to be sixty-five, I might say 'get an endowment,' although I've never sold one.

"But you see, I don't have a crystal ball. But I *do* know that ordinary life is the greatest amount of life insurance you can buy . . . for the least amount of money . . . with a guaranteed return of your money.

"So if you get nothing more out of this interview, young man, remember ordinary life."

I pause just a moment before I give him the third question.

"*When* should you buy it? . . . Right now!

"Why *now?* . . . Let's go back to when we talked about how much you should buy. I said an amount you can *easily* afford . . . So there's no reason to delay.

"Last question: From whom should you buy?"

Again, I pause slightly before I tell him, "Well, I'm not here promoting the Metropolitan!"

Once in a while the young man will tell me he thinks maybe he ought to do business with one of those *big* companies. And I always tell him, "Son, if size were the most important thing, Miss America would weigh 400 pounds!"

Sometimes, too, I've used the following spiel to impress upon the prospect the wisdom of buying from me: (If I used it now, the figures would have to be revised.)

I would tell the prospect, "There are 1700 agents licensed to sell life insurance in Metropolitan Toledo and the outlying areas. I happen to be one of the 1700.

"Now, of the 1700 agents, 375 belong to the National Association of Life Underwriters. I happen to be one of the 375.

"Of the 375 members, 39 are also members of the Million Dollar Round Table. I happen to be one of the 39.

"Of those 39, 21 sold over two million dollars worth of business in the city of Toledo. I happen to be one of the 21.

"Of the 21 in Toledo, nine sold over three million last year; I happen to be one of the nine. Of the nine, four sold over four million; I happen to be one of the four. And of the four, one sold over five million.

"I happen to be the one."

(Again, these figures would have to be revised if I were to use this spiel now. For one thing, I'm certainly not the only agent in the Toledo area producing over five million.)

Idea #2
Family Situation
"Economic Circle of Life"

I've sold more insurance with this idea than any other idea I've ever had. I first got the basis of the idea from Bill Warnkin (of Columbus Mutual, working out of Cleveland). Then later at the Million Dollar Round Table meeting, Price Ripley (of National Life of Vermont) gave me more ideas that were added to the original. And, finally, I embellished upon these ideas to come up with the complete idea you see here.

This is a family situation with three or four children. I'm talking to the husband and wife. (I have done this in a home at the dining room table, with a mere sheet of paper for illustration purposes. Ninety percent of the time, as you know, I have the interviews in my office.)

I draw one large circle on the board (Fig. 1). As I'm doing it, I tell them that anytime during the interview they think I'm out of line with my requests, just tell me . . . and I'll erase the blackboard, and we'll talk about sports or something else.

I then ask them the name of their family doctor. They tell me, and I then mark an X on the top of the circle, and write in the doctor's name. (Fig. 1, #1) If it's a young couple, I frequently ask for the name of their pediatrician, and add another X and put his name down. (Fig. 1, #2)

Then, I ask for the name of their dentist, and put a third X with his name (Fig. 1, #3).

I ask them a very important question—the name of their attorney . . . because if they *don't* have one, the sale is made.

You see, if they don't have an attorney, they don't have a will. And if they don't have a will in a state that is governed by the two-thirds/one-third distribution rule, they definitely need

IDEA #2

Figure 1

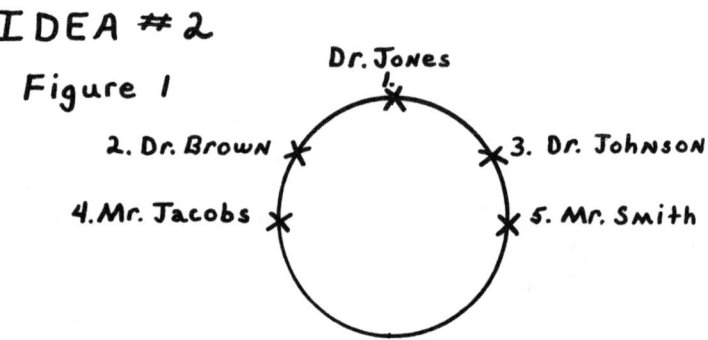

Dr. Jones 1.
2. Dr. Brown
3. Dr. Johnson
4. Mr. Jacobs
5. Mr. Smith

Figure 2

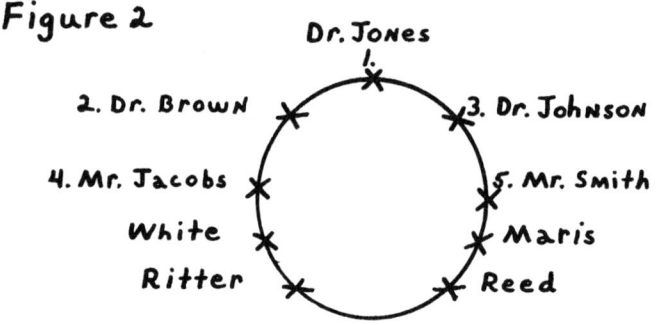

Dr. Jones 1.
2. Dr. Brown
3. Dr. Johnson
4. Mr. Jacobs
5. Mr. Smith
White
Maris
Ritter
Reed

Figure 3

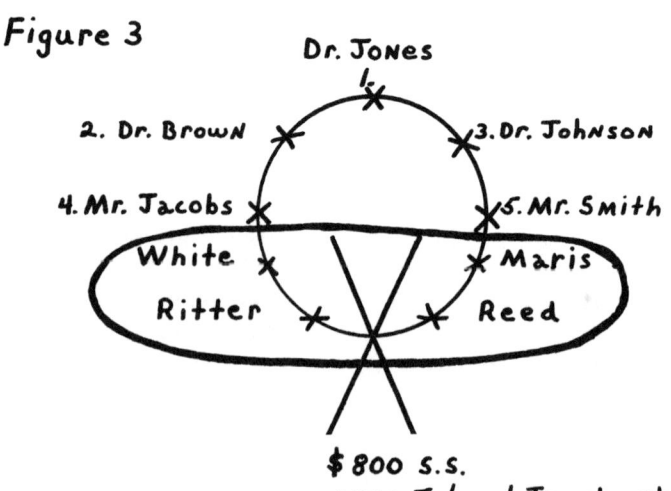

Dr. Jones 1.
2. Dr. Brown
3. Dr. Johnson
4. Mr. Jacobs
5. Mr. Smith
White
Maris
Ritter
Reed

$800 S.S.
1,200 Interest Investment Proceeds
$2,000 Family Need

a will. After I help them in this area, I will gain their complete confidence.

(By the way, I make sure *every one* of my clients has a will or a trust agreement.)

But let's say they have an attorney. I put another X and write his name (Fig. 1, # 4).

"Who is your auto and fire insurance agent?" I'll ask next. And they'll give me, say, Bill Smith of Safe Form. And I enter his name (Fig. 1, # 5).

"Now that I've been giving so much attention to everybody else and helping them out, I finally get to the important part of the circle—life insurance."

(And this is where you really practice your art of selling. Know your merchandise, know policy provisions, and know the companies you're competing with.)

I'll ask them for their policies (if it's an office interview, I always make sure they bring them). I open all the policies up, and fold each back to the application portion of the contract.

And, if you're guessing that there are often as many different agents as there are policies, you're right. For example's sake, let's say four policies—four names.

I then go to the bottom of my circle (Fig. 2), and one by one, put a small X and the name of each agent that appears on each policy.

Then I step back from the board and ask them, "Is there anything unusual about that picture? . . . You have a professional man here, here, (and I point to each name) here, here, and here. But in this area (I point to the life insurance set of X's and names)—where you probably spend more money than all the other areas put together—you *don't* have a professional man . . . I'm applying for the job!"

(As I say this, I circle the four X's and names, and put a large X through it.) (Fig. 3).

Notice that I haven't talked about cash values, about dividends, about net payments or net cost. All I've talked about adds up to "psychologically baking a cake" one-on-one.

One of the couple—usually the one who is *not* your prime target, and usually the wife—will say something like "Boy, Harry, that sure makes sense to me."

I want to tell you that if it makes sense to *her* and it makes sense to *me*, old Harry's in trouble! There's no way he's going to get out of this . . . because now it's *two-on-one!*

But often Harry will say something like, "You don't expect me to get rid of all my policies and buy yours, do you?"

And I'll answer, "No. The best policies are the ones you have right now—the ones you already bought!"

And he's glad to hear this.

(But that isn't the only reason I say it. I happen to believe that we in the insurance business don't have to make our livings as scavengers, by taking other policies and other premiums on policies.)

I explain to him that the job I'm applying for is to coordinate his total program, and with Social Security benefits, arrive at the dollars needed to take care of his family.

Then alongside the circle (Fig. 3) I explain with simple computation how he can leave his family $2,000 a month. (Based on a man earning $2,000 now—after taxes—and based on the idea that he should leave this amount to his family if he dies).

I show him that Social Security will leave his family $800 a month, and that $170,000 worth of life insurance will bear interest— if invested prudently—of $1,200 a month. (Fig. 3).

(I never deplete the insurance principal in a program.)

Idea #3

"For the Single Young Man Who Doesn't Need Insurance"
Situation A

I use this basis presentation idea for two situations. (Situation B is Idea #4) But it comes out a little differently each time.

This is where a young man already has insurance, and his insurance-need situation hasn't changed. Maybe he bought a couple of years ago when he was in college, and now he's out and has a job but he's still not married. (Let's say he previously bought a $25,000 policy ... from me or somebody else— makes no difference.)

He's in my office, we're just talking insurance in general terms, and he asks me if he really needs any more insurance.

I tell him "no" and he's relieved. That's exactly what he wanted to hear.

I tell him, "If you die, your family gets rich."

(I draw an illustration, Figure 1, as I continue talking.)

I write the word "Single" (Fig. 2) as I say, "But tell me, is there a possibility that you're going to get married some day?"

And the guy tells me that it sure is possible.

"Well," I say, "Let's say you get married here. (I write the word in Fig. 2). Would you say you'd need life insurance at this point?"

The young man agrees.

IDEA #3

Figure 1

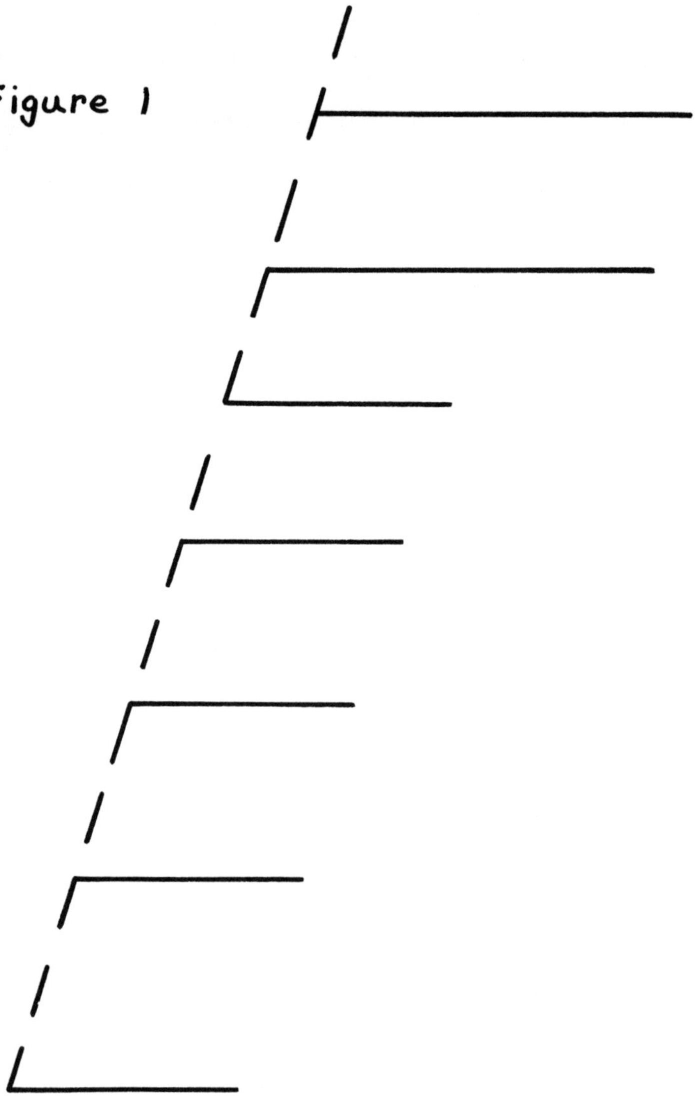

Figure 2

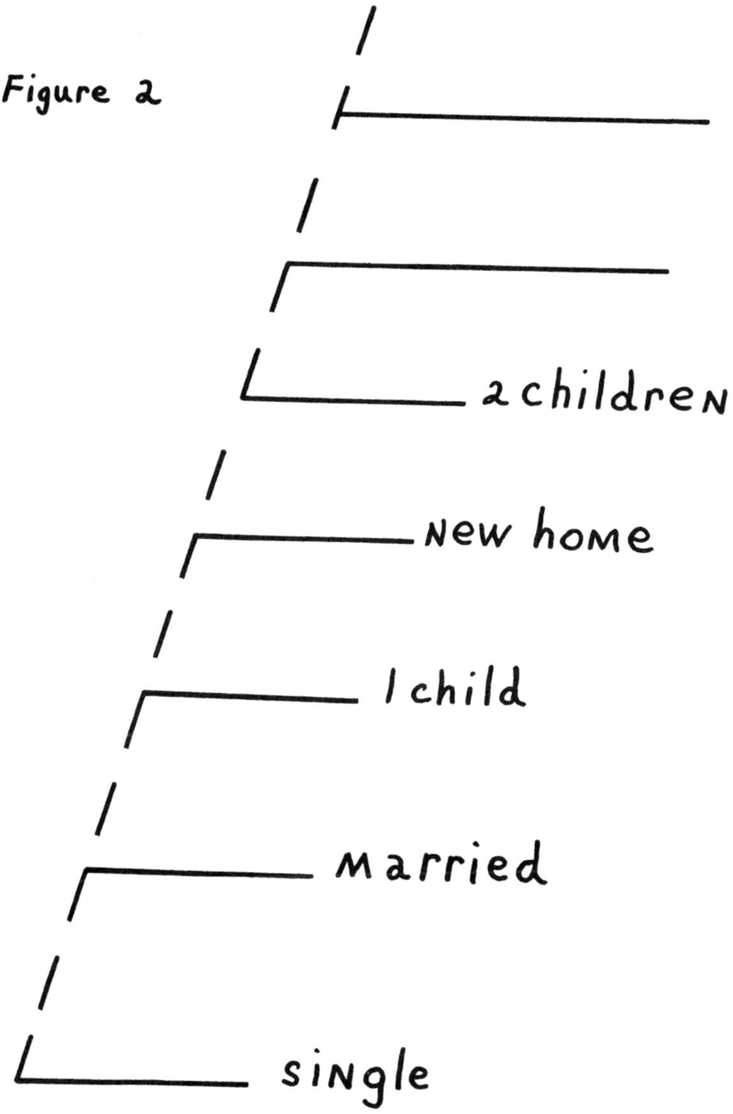

2 children

New home

I child

Married

single

I continue, "And let's say you have a child here. (I mark the word in the figure.) Would you agree you'd need even more insurance at that point?"

Again he agrees.

I continue, taking him as far up the line as I think necessary until I finally say, "Then I want to tell you something; buy it now! Because the rate will then be level for the rest of your life." (I point to the bottom line in Fig. 2.)

"It won't keep going up every time the economy changes, (I point to the broken line) . . . and every time you get older (I point again to the broken line) . . . and every time you take on another responsibility." (I point to the horizontal lines, beginning with the "married" line.)

"Proportionately it will become cheaper, won't it? Because while everything else goes up—including your income—your life insurance premium is going to stay the same. In fact, it will go *down*, with the dividends you earn."

"You see, life insurance costs you less to buy today than it will any time in the future!"

Idea #4

"For the Single Young Man Who Doesn't Need Insurance"

Situation B

This is where the single young man has never purchased insurance before, and he and his family both figure he doesn't need insurance. The presentation here takes on a variation from Situation A—especially where you have to deal with the father and mother in addition to the young man.

After my opening monolog, I get quickly to the business at hand.

"Mr. Jones, I want to talk to Jerry about his life insurance coverage. But I want to be educational. So let's pick my brain apart—based on the experience I've had. I'm just going to throw out some things to you . . .

"Number one, a boy his age *doesn't need life insurance.* Not only doesn't he need it, he doesn't even *want* it!"

The father sits there pleased as punch. That's exactly what he wanted to hear. He's relieved.

I continue, "If he dies, the only ones who are going to benefit are his parents—and it's going to be a windfall for them. There's no need factor here. There's no protection factor here because it costs very little to bury someone.

"And I've found—and this is very interesting—a guy gets married. He has a good job. And he's making $25,000 a year."

I stop, and say, "But let's back up. Jerry, do you think that some day you'll make $25,000?"

And the young man says yes. (There's not a young guy alive who doesn't think he'll make $25,000 some day.)

(Now, I might or might not use the illustration I used in Idea # 3)

"Do you think someday you'll get married?" (Yes) "Do you think someday you'll have a family?" (Yes)

(And so forth, as far as necessary.)

"Now, if you do all these things, you're going to need life insurance. I'm sure everyone will agree with that.

"You bring home $25,000 a year, and you die coming home; you've got to have something for your wife and kids."

The father and mother are both nodding yes to that.

"Now, the guy who's looking ahead will get some insurance now—even though he doesn't need it—because it's never going to cost less than when you buy it now.

"That's the main reason to buy it now. And the second reason is because there's no assurance that when you get to this position that you can buy it. You could be eliminated by a health factor.

"But the *worst* thing you can do is to become insurance poor. The worst thing you can do is to buy a lot of life insurance now."

(And you say this to eliminate the tons of objections that come down the road.)

"What you should buy is an amount you can easily afford."

(And sometimes I go into the basics of Idea # 1)

Idea #5
Decreasing Term Mortgage Insurance
The Wrong Product to Sell

This is another of those ideas I developed during an actual interview. I had never done it before; it just popped into my mind. I did it, and it worked!

And I'm so excited about it, I can hardly wait to get to my next appointment! I'm like the baseball player who can hit the pitcher. I'm so anxious, I want to beat the bat up to the plate!

The idea can be used in the situation where a family already has decreasing term mortgage insurance . . . or where a family wants to buy such a policy. Many times you'll find that the couple has already discussed decreasing term with someone who advocates it, so they're pretty much set in their own minds, maybe, that it's the way to buy mortgage insurance.

In my opinion—as you'll soon see—I think that this kind of buying is as antiquated as the hoop skirt. And I think you have to convince the client of this, in a positive way, if you're really going to do the job for him.

(By the way, you should know that some of the banks and some of the savings and loan companies are going into the mortgage insurance business . . . but I love it! I think it's easy to sell against the competition we now have. Do you realize how much easier it'll be against guys who don't know anything! Animal crackers and duck soup!)

I draw a home (the smaller house in Fig. 1) on the blackboard. (And the way I draw, I many times have to remind the clients that that's what it is.)

I'll tell the couple, "Now, you bought your home six years ago, and you probably bought mortgage insurance at that time."

IDEA #5

Figure 1

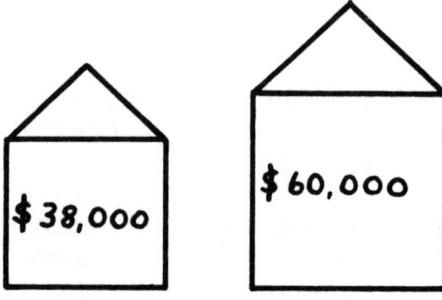

$38,000 $60,000

Figure 2

INSURANCE

Figure 3

ECONOMY
INSURANCE

Figure 4

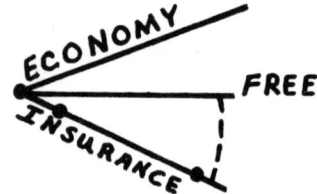

ECONOMY
INSURANCE
FREE

I ask the guy then, "Do you have mortgage insurance?"

(Now, if he doesn't have it, that's a sale. And if he does have it, that's better. I mean, no matter what he says, there's going to be a sale made!)

I continue, "When you bought the insurance to protect your mortgage (I draw a line and write in 'insurance'—see Fig. 2), your mortgage was $38,000 (I place a dot at the top of the line).

"Now, your mortgage is $34,000. (I make another dot farther down.) I just want you to travel this mortgage route with me. What do you think is going to happen when this mortgage gets down to $5,000 (I draw a third and final dot) . . . or it's eliminated completely?" (I merely point to the bottom of the line.)

The couple invariably tell me, "We're going to get another house."

Then I ask them, "Is the house going to be bigger or smaller than the one you now have?"

They invariably answer, "Bigger." (I draw another of my houses—go back up to Fig. 1.)

Then I ask, "Is the new mortgage going to be bigger or smaller than the old one?" (Obviously, I know what their answer is going to be.)

I continue, "Now, your mortgage is going to be bigger, and this policy by that time is down to here." (Point to wherever you choose on the insurance line—Fig. 2.)

"So here's the economy line (I start from the top of the insurance line and draw a line at an acute angle to the insurance line and label it "economy"—Fig. 3), and here's your insurance (I point again to the insurance line). You'd better die soon . . . because each year you wait, the worse off you're going to be! . . . Because the economy is running away from you!

"Now, it's the same thing with this mortgage on the house. When ten years from now it's down (point to insurance line), you're going to go get a bigger house with a bigger mortgage (point to larger house in Fig. 1 and mark the amount). And let's say it's a $60,000 home.

"Then, what do you think is going to happen to your present policy? There's no provision—I just checked it out—they won't allow you to go up to $60,000."

The couple may say something like, "They won't?"

And I'll say "Uh-uh."

Then I'll pause, and look at the young couple, and say, "I'm so happy that I came here . . . because I have a tremendous solution for you!

"What if I brought your mortgage insurance from this line (I point to the insurance line) to this line? (I draw a third line in the middle.) Because I can do that *free*." (And I draw a broken line and write the word "Free." Now my illustration looks like Fig. 4.)

I point again to the illustration as I repeat, "I can take it from this line to this line free . . . if you'll take it the rest of the way for $60 a month." (I trace an imaginary line from the middle line up to the top of the economy line.)

"You see, the cost of decreasing term insurance, plus the dividends off the other life insurance that you have, will buy *level* term insurance. And $60 additional will buy ordinary life, with paid up additions."

(How you say this and how you handle yourself here is major league or it's minor league—you've got to perfect your art.) I continue, "Your insurance program will be increasing and when you go from this house to this house (I point to the houses — Fig. 1) you're going to be in good shape."

Idea #6
For The Successful Person

Here's an idea the younger agent can use on the older successful man. You can draw the circles on a blackboard or a piece of paper.

(I point to the top circle and say to the prospect.)

"How are you here?"

(The successful prospect always tells you that he is in good shape and gives you some details about his personal insurance program.)

(Point to the center circle and say to the prospect.)

"How are you here?"

(Generally I get the same answer, I'm in good shape. Frequently I'll get the details about the buy out plan, pension, profit-sharing, etc.)

(Then, pointing to the bottom circle, I ask the prospect.)

"How are you here?

"What is a capital tax?

"That's a tax that the government levies when you're in good shape in the other two areas!"

IDEA #6

FAMILY
INSURANCE

BUSINESS
INSURANCE

CAPITAL
TAX

Idea #7
"The Procrastinator"

Sometimes when I read the young man to be reluctant to buy *now*, I tell him a little story.

I start out by drawing a half-circle (Figure 1.)

I tell the young man, "I drew this for you because half of the people in this country fall into this category. I know you'll be bright enough to understand why you shouldn't belong there.

"Several years ago I had an interview with a young man just out of high school. He told me he didn't want to buy just then; he wanted a little time to get his feet on the ground.

"So I said 'yes' and agreed to wait a while."

(I say "yes" to everything. I operate like an undertaker; I feel I'm eventually going to get most of them anyway.)

I continue telling the prospect my story. "So the first year he doesn't get into the program. And he doesn't save any money that year, either." (I mark the first zero at the bottom of the semicircle. Fig. 2)

"A year later, I call him up, and he comes in for another interview. He tells me he's doing just fine, but he's changing jobs and as soon as he gets settled into it, he'll do business. I tell him 'Fine.' And that took care of another year." (I add another zero to Fig. 2).

"Next year—another interview. This time he is engaged to be married . . . wants to wait just until after the wedding; then we'd be able to sit down together and plan the whole thing out." (I add a third zero.)

IDEA # 7

Figure 1

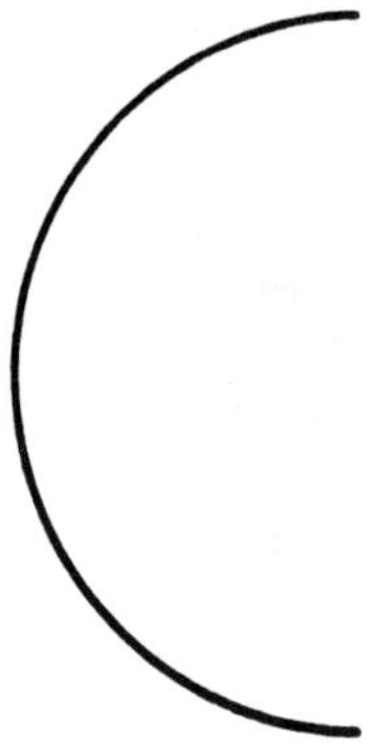

Figure 2

Figure 3

"The next year, it is a baby on the way, with no way he can see clear to put anything away for now." (I mark another zero.)

"And the year after that, it is buying a new home, with the thought that by the next year he'd be in fine shape to start his insurance program." (I mark the final zero.)

I turn to the young man and say, "You see, there's just never a convenient time to buy."

I let that sink in, before I go on.

"You see how foolish he is. First of all, he doesn't know when he's going to die. If he had that going for him he wouldn't need me!

"Second, by the time he's ready to buy, no company may want him—because he may be uninsurable!"

Then I refer to Figure 3 again, and say, "And do you see what this man wasted? What he could have bought for X (I mark an X in Fig. 3) will now cost him Y." (I mark a Y.)

"And you know the really sad thing is that I only wanted him to put away $10 a month."

Idea #8
For The Recently Married
Young Couple

This is more for a couple who has little or no savings, usually with just a modest income. The young man is twenty-three years old, let's say.

I draw two lines on the blackboard (Figure 1) for the couple, and ask the young man how much he's making a year. Let's say his answer is around the $12,000 figure. (I write in the amount—and his age opposite it—on the bottom line—Fig. 2.)

I look at his wife, and then him, and say, "Project, if you will, to the time when you'll be forty-three years old." (I draw the slant line and mark in the age on the top line—Fig. 2.)

"How much money do you think you'll be making?" I ask him.

He thinks for a few seconds, and let's say he answers with a figure around $30,000 a year.

I say, "Well, let's drop that down a little bit. I always like to work positive. Let's make it $25,000, O.K.?"

He nods, and I put the amount on the top line (Fig. 2).

I say then, "Young man, there's only one thing that's going to keep you from making $25,000 at age 43."

He looks at me and usually says something like, "What's that?"

And I say, "If you don't get there." (And I erase "Age 43"—Fig. 3.)

IDEA # 8

Figure 1

_____

_____

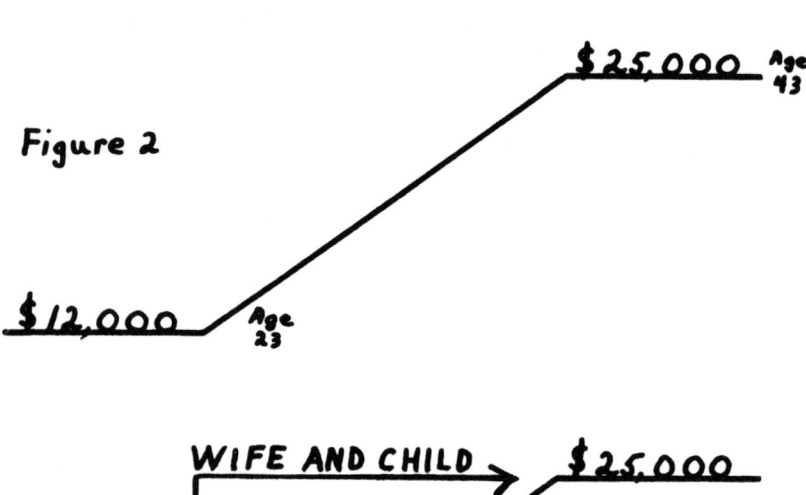

Figure 2

$25,000 Age 43

$12,000 Age 23

Figure 3

WIFE AND CHILD → $25,000

$12,000 Age 23

"Now think about this," I continue. (And I draw the perforated vertical line and the horizontal arrowed line—Fig. 3.) "Here's your wife and child (I write in the words—Fig. 3). I don't want your wife and child not to make it . . . just because you failed to make it.

"If you buy a fair amount of life insurance, you can assure them that their income is going to be provided, whether you make it or not."

(One cautionary note: This is a logical explanation, not an emotional appeal. Don't be maudlin or dramatic in your references to the guy "not making it." It's a fact of life, not something to sentimentalize them into action. They'll resent it later if you do.)

Idea #9
Estate Planning With The Family

Don't get carried away with the estate plan. It's really very simple. If a Phys. Ed. major can get it, anyone can.

I'll say to the man, "How much could your family get by on?"

And let's say he'll say around $1,500 a month, and let's say I discovered earlier in the interview that he's making $2,000 net a month.

I ask him where he's putting his $500 savings each month. And he tells me, "John, we don't save a dime."

I repeat it, "You don't save a dime? Let me ask you a couple of questions.

"In the last five years have you ever had a pay raise?" And he says, "Why sure."

And I say, "Let me ask you this then. In the next five years if you didn't get a pay raise, would you be unhappy?" And again he says, "Why sure."

I tell him, "You know, you're sort of an amazing guy. *You* would be unhappy without a pay raise, but you're seemingly satisfied for your wife to take a pay cut!"

(And if he's big, you smile! Right away! Don't delay! One thing you don't need is a big hulk of a guy reaching across the desk and grabbing you!)

I explain quickly. "You said you need $2,000 a month, because you're making $2,000 and not saving any. Now that means if you die, your family still needs $2,000 a month . . . and I know how you can do it real simple."

121

IDEA #9

COMPUTATION:

$800 S.S.
1200 NEED
$2,000 TOTAL NEED

Figure 1

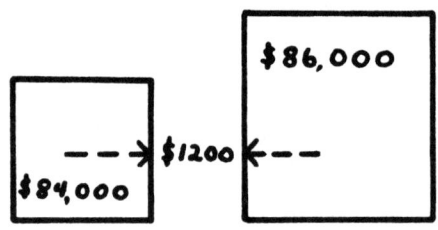

Figure 2

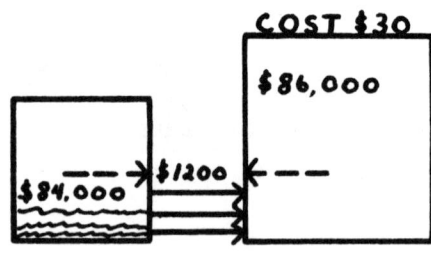

(I'll draw a line and write the $2,000 figure below it and label it—see "Computation" on the illustration).

He asks me what I mean, and I tell him . . .

"Social Security is going to give you $800 (I deal in approximate numbers whenever I can). You need another $1,200, right?"

(I write these figures and label them as I say them—see "Computation" again).

"I've observed by going over your total program, you own $84,000. (I draw what you could refer to as two bank vaults, and write in the figures—Fig. 1) So you only need $86,000 more."

They both look quizzically at me and I explain. "$86,000 plus $84,000 is $170,000. The interest from $170,000 will give you the $1,200 you need each month . . . and the principal will never be touched."

(I draw perforated arrows from the vaults and write $800— Fig. 1).

Then I pause and add matter-of-factly, "And, you know, you can get the $86,000 for $30 a month."

(I write "Cost $30"—Fig. 2).

The man is usually the one to speak up. "What do you mean — $30?" he says. "I'm paying $75 a month for the $84,000!"

I say, "I didn't ask you what you were paying. I said you can get the additional $86,000 for $30 per month."

"What I'll do is take the dividends off of all your existing coverage. (I draw the wavy lines and the three arrows—Fig. 2.) I take those dollars I need per month to go with your $30 . . . to buy $86,000 worth of insurance—even if it's all term."

You see, I don't care how much term insurance I have to sell the client. I'll build him up *eventually* with ordinary life . . . but I can't build him up if I don't have him. (You can't have rabbit stew unless you catch the rabbit!) And if that's all he can afford, he needs the coverage!

I sell lots of term. I sold around a million dollars worth last year. (As I said before, I sell insurance *first* as a *protection* vehicle.) But I also sold four or five of ordinary. Neither one is bad, right?

Another aspect is the beneficiary provisions of the policy, or a trust agreement.

If you really want to look out for the family, make sure that the wife and kids are not left a lump sum to fritter away (if the husband sees it this way, too).

Example, the wife gets $50,000. She spends it instead of investing it and supplementing it with earnings.

You've hurt her and the family by putting them into a position where they can be foolish.

Potpourri

Nothing Fancy

When I sell life insurance I don't use a thing except a blackboard and a pad of paper. It's terrible, but I often have to ask for the use of a pen.

Do you have all three?

For a person to succeed in this business you have to have three things:

(1) Guts

(2) Hard work

(3) Intelligence

If a person has any two out of these three, *he will fail.* A man *must* have all three. If any one area is left out, there is just no way that he can make it.

They'll come to your office.

In 1966 I went to bed for nine months but I still had to support my family. So, I asked people to come to see me in the hospital. I sold $3,500,000 in 1966.

That taught me that people would come to me.

Today I have all of my closing appointments in my office and even our new agents have 80 per cent of their closing appointments in the office.